LOCAL RED BOOK

DUNDEE ST ANDREW

CARNOUSTIE • CUPAR • LEUCH

CONTENTS

Page Layout & Road Map — **2**
3 Miles to 1 Inch

Dundee Enlarged Centre — **3**
8 Inches to 1 Mile

Street Maps — **4-29**
4 Inches to 1 Mile

Index to Streets — **30**

Red Books showing the way

Every effort has been made to verify the accuracy of information in this book but the publishers cannot accept responsibility for expense or loss caused by an error or omission.

Information that will be of assistance to the user of the maps will be welcomed.

The representation on these maps of a road, track or path is no evidence of the existence of a right of way.

Street plans prepared and published by ESTATE PUBLICATIONS, Bridewell House, TENTERDEN, KENT. The Publishers acknowledge the co-operation of the local authorities of towns represented in this atlas.

Ordnance Survey® This product includes mapping data licensed from Ordnance Survey® with the permission of the Controller of Her Majesty's Stationery Office.

652-02/04-05
ISBN 1 84192 398 2

www.ESTATE-PUBLICATIONS.co.uk

LEGEN

Motorwa
Track
Built Up A
Footpath
Stream
River
Canal
Railway /
Post Offic
Car Park / Park & Ri
Public Co
Place of W
One-way
Tourist Inf Centre
Adjoining
Area Depi Enlarged
Emergenc
Industrial
Leisure Bu
Education
Hotels etc
Retail Buil
General B
Woodland
Orchard
Recreation Parkland
Cemetery

D LAYOUT & ROAD MAP

Scale: 3 Miles to 1 Inch

oute
Road.

d

zed /
Access

rea

Station

e
venience
orship
treet
ormation

Pages
ting
entre
y Services
Buildings
ildings
Buildings

ings
ildings

al /

DUNDEE
Firth of Tay
TAY ROAD BRIDGE
A92
Toll Bridge
Victoria Dock
North Carr Lightship
Apex Hotel
Port of Dundee Offices
CITY QUAY SHOPPING CENTRE
EAST DOCK ST
EAST DOCK RD RETAIL PARK
MARKETGAIT
EAST MARKETGAIT
WEST MARKETGAIT
NORTH MARKETGAIT
SEAGATE
EAST WHALE LANE
Sports Centre
PRINCES ST
KING STREET
A929
Day Centre
Bus Station
TRADES LANE
Multi Storey
St Peters Cathedral
Caird Town Hall
CITY SQUARE
Tayside House
Casino
Hilton Hotel
Craig Harbour
RRS Discovery
Discovery Point
Olympia Leisure Centre
SOUTH UNION STREET
RIVERSIDE DRIVE
A85
Hotel
MURRAYGATE
COMMERCIAL ST
CASTLE ST
HIGH STREET
CRICHTON STREET
THE WELLGATE SHOPPING CENTRE
Library
Steps Theatre
VICTORIA ROAD
A90
HILLTOWN
MEADOWSIDE
McManus Galleries & Museum
FORUM SHOPPING CENTRE
Market
NEW INN ENTRY
OVERGATE SHOPPING CENTRE
St Marys Tower
The Old Steeple
NETHERGATE
NETHERGATE BUSINESS CENTRE
Bingo Hall
Caledonian House
The Howff Graveyard
School
University of Abertay
Restricted Access
Cathedral
Arts Centre
Sensation Science Centre
Rep Theatre
Bonar Hall
Caird House
Mill
Multi Storey
University
Tayside Police HQ
Courts
Wedderburn Building
Dundee College
Scrymgeour Building & Law Library
Carnelley Building
Tower
Ewing Building
Fulton Building
Harris Building
Carnegie Building
Library
UNIVERSITY OF DUNDEE
Students Association & Swimming Pool
Airlie Hall
Crawford Building
Belmont Hall
Duncan of Jordanstone College
Mathew Building
Institute of Sport & Exercise
PERTH ROAD
HAWKHILL
B911
Verdant Works Museum
Bowling Club
Dudhope Castle
Dudhope Park
LOCHEE ROAD
A923
BLINSHALL STREET
BROWN STREET
WEST HENDERSONS WYND
PERTH ROAD
Seabraes
1
2
3
4
A
B
C
D
E
F
14
15

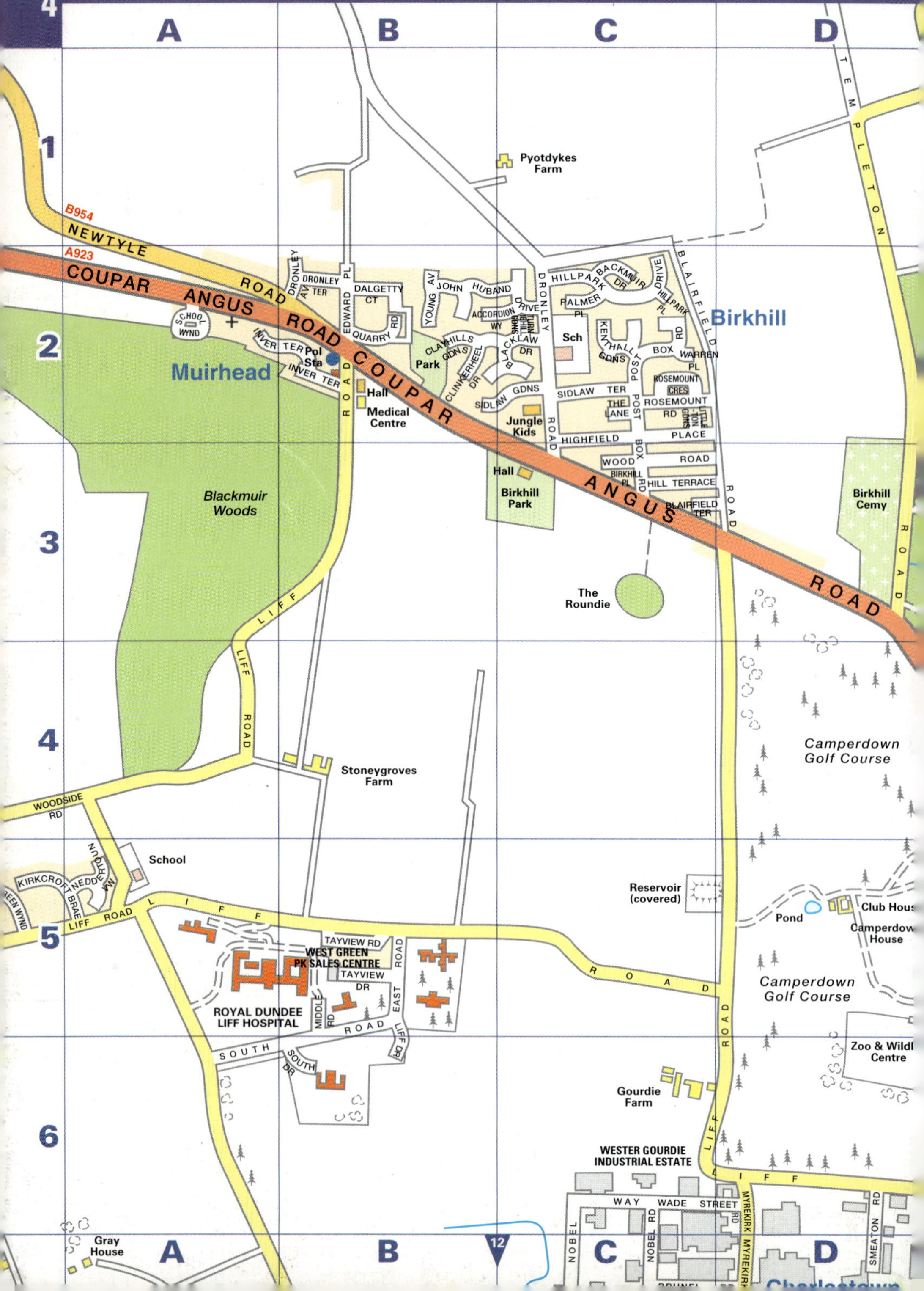
A
B
C
D
1
2
3
4
5
6
B954
NEWTYLE ROAD
A923
COUPAR ANGUS ROAD
Pyotdykes Farm
Muirhead
Birkhill
SCHOOL WYND
DRONLEY AV
DRONLEY TER
EDWARD PL
DALGETTY CT
QUARRY RD
YOUNG AV
JOHN HUBAND DRIVE
ACCORDION WY
DRONLEY ROAD
HILLPARK DR
BACKMUIR DRIVE
HILLPARK PL
BLAIRFIELD ROAD
PALMER PL
Sch
KENTHALL GDNS
BOX
WARREN PL
ROSEMOUNT CRES
ROSEMOUNT RD
SIDLAW TER
THE LANE
POST
LITTLETON GDNS
PLACE
HIGHFIELD
WOOD
ROAD
BIRKHILL PL
HILL TERRACE
BLAIRFIELD TER
CLAYHILLS GDNS
CLINKERHEEL DR
BLACKLAW DR
SIDLAW GDNS
Park
INVER TER
Pol Sta
Hall
Medical Centre
Jungle Kids
Birkhill Park
Blackmuir Woods
The Roundie
Birkhill Cemy
LIFF ROAD
Camperdown Golf Course
Stoneygroves Farm
WOODSIDE RD
School
KIRKCROFT
NEDDERTOUN VW
BRAE
GREEN WYND
TAYVIEW RD
WEST GREEN PK SALES CENTRE
TAYVIEW DR
EAST ROAD
MIDDLE RD
ROYAL DUNDEE LIFF HOSPITAL
SOUTH ROAD
SOUTH DR
LIFF DR
Reservoir (covered)
Pond
Gourdie Farm
WESTER GOURDIE INDUSTRIAL ESTATE
WAY
WADE STREET
NOBEL RD
MYREKIRK RD
SMEATON RD
Gray House
12

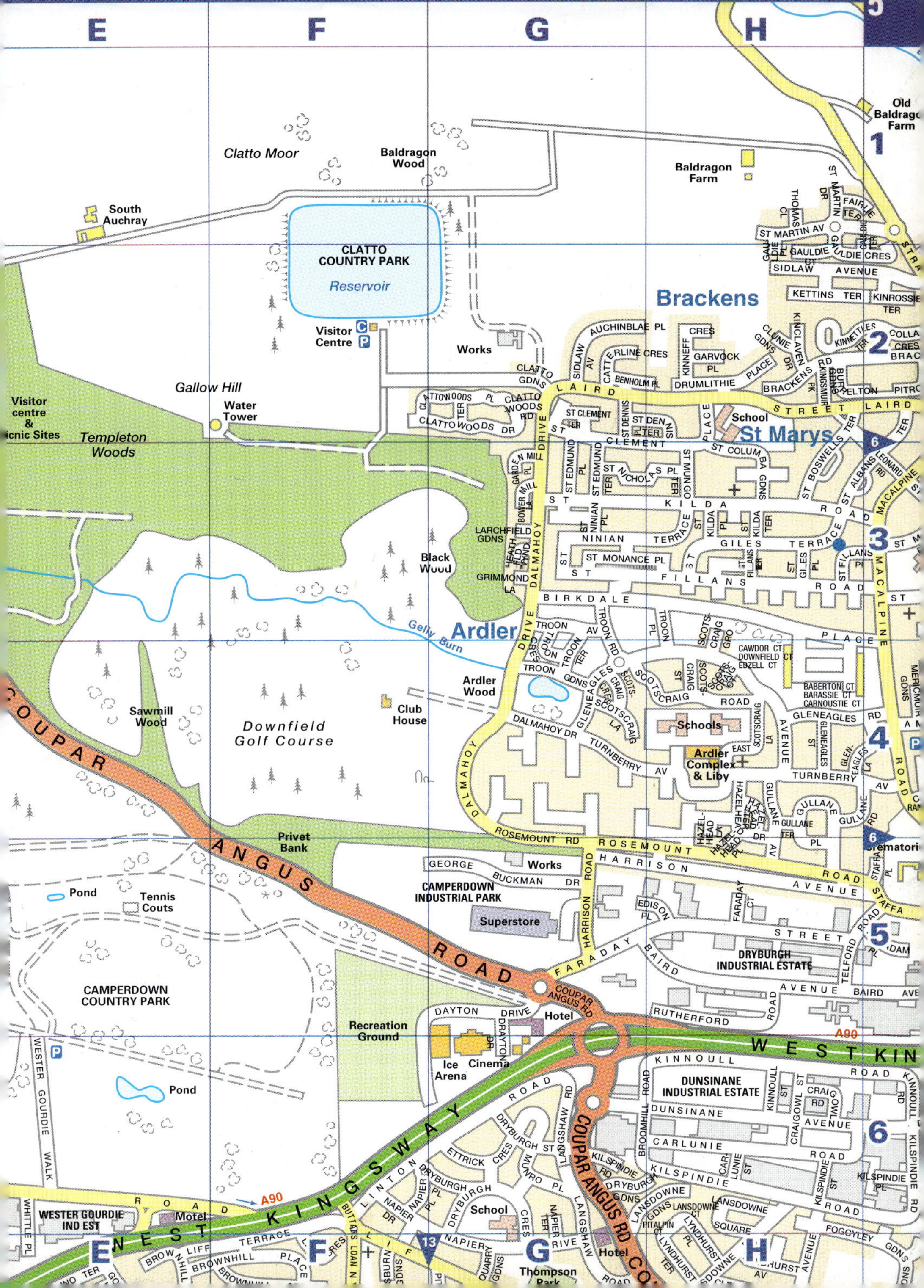

E
F
G
H
1
2
3
4
5
6
Clatto Moor
Baldragon Wood
Old Baldragon Farm
Baldragon Farm
South Auchray
CLATTO COUNTRY PARK
Reservoir
Visitor Centre
Works
Gallow Hill
Water Tower
Visitor centre & Picnic Sites
Templeton Woods
Brackens
St Marys
School
Black Wood
Ardler
Gelly Burn
Ardler Wood
Club House
Sawmill Wood
Downfield Golf Course
Schools
Ardler Complex & Liby
COUPAR ANGUS ROAD
Privet Bank
Pond
Tennis Couts
CAMPERDOWN COUNTRY PARK
CAMPERDOWN INDUSTRIAL PARK
Superstore
Works
DRYBURGH INDUSTRIAL ESTATE
Recreation Ground
Hotel
Ice Arena
Cinema
DUNSINANE INDUSTRIAL ESTATE
WEST KINGSWAY
A90
WESTER GOURDIE IND EST
Motel
School
Hotel
Thompson Park
Crematorium
AUCHINBLAE PL
CATTERLINE CRES
BENHOLM PL
KINNEFF CRES
GARVOCK PL
DRUMLITHIE PLACE
BRACKENS RD
LAIRD STREET
ST MARTIN AV
GAULDIE CRES
SIDLAW AVENUE
KETTINS TER
KINROSSIE TER
CLATTO GDNS
CLATTOWOODS PL
CLATTOWOODS DR
ST CLEMENT TER
ST DENNIS TER
ST COLUMBA GDNS
ST BOSWELLS TER
ST KILDA ROAD
ST KILDA TERRACE
ST NINIAN TERRACE
ST MONANCE PL
ST GILES TERRACE
ST FILLANS ROAD
MACALPINE ROAD
LARCHFIELD GDNS
GRIMMOND LA
DALMAHOY DRIVE
BIRKDALE PLACE
TROON AV
SCOTSCRAIG ROAD
GLENEAGLES RD
CAWDOR CT
DOWNFIELD CT
EDZELL CT
BABERTON CT
BARASSIE CT
CARNOUSTIE CT
TURNBERRY AV
GULLANE AV
DALMAHOY DR
ROSEMOUNT RD
HARRISON ROAD
HARRISON AVENUE
GEORGE BUCKMAN DR
EDISON PL
FARADAY STREET
BAIRD AVENUE
TELFORD ROAD
RUTHERFORD ROAD
STAFFA PL
DAYTON DRIVE
DRAYTON DR
KINNOULL ROAD
DUNSINANE AVENUE
CARLUNIE ROAD
KILSPINDIE ROAD
CRAIGOWL AVENUE
LANSDOWNE SQUARE
FOGGYLEY GDNS
BROOMHILL ROAD
DRYBURGH GDNS
LINTON ROAD
ETTRICK CRES
MUNRO PL
LANGSHAW RD
NAPIER DRIVE
BROWNHILL PLACE
BUTTARS LOAN
WESTER GOURDIE WALK
WHITTLE PL
6
13

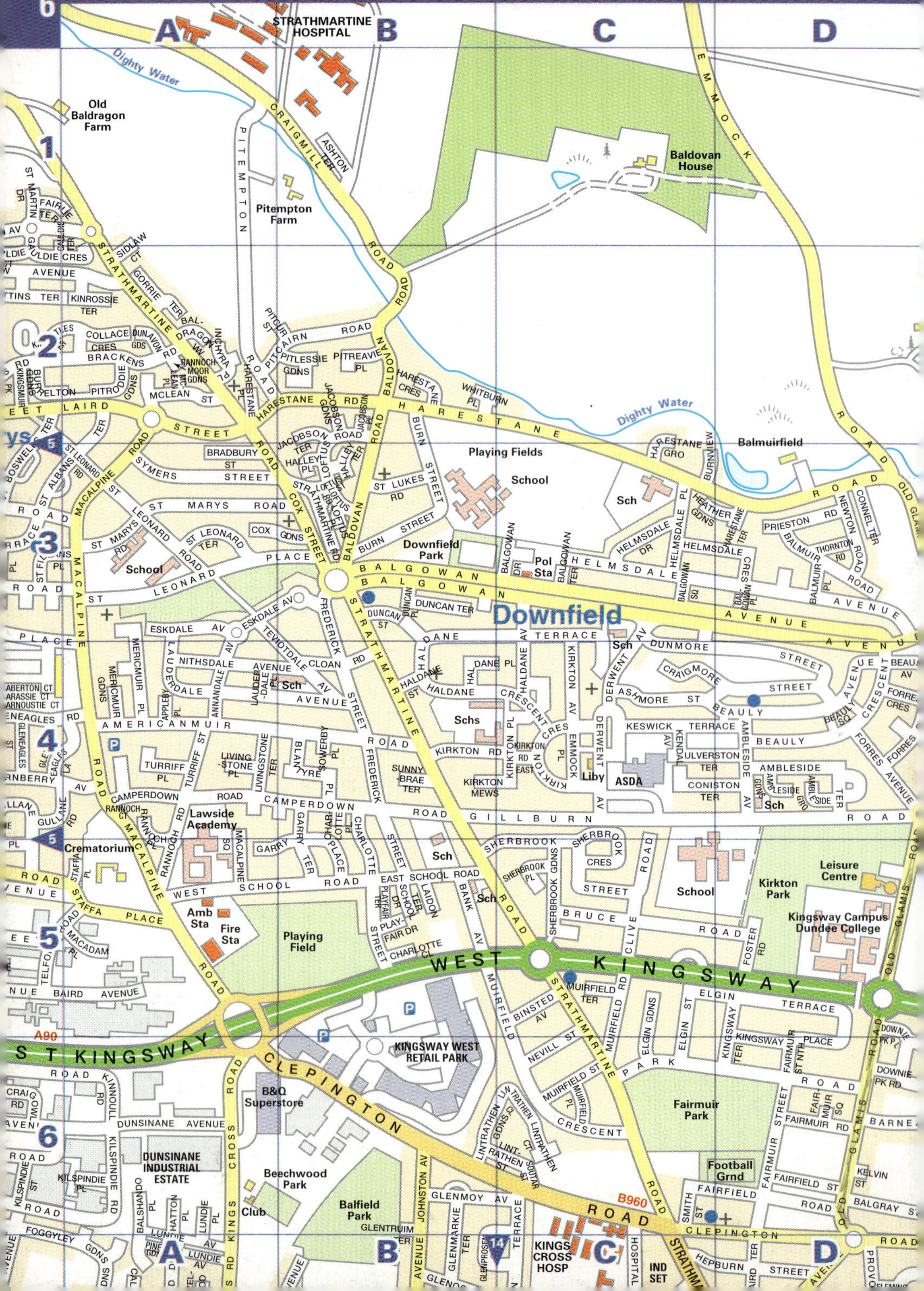
STRATHMARTINE HOSPITAL
Old Baldragon Farm
Pitempton Farm
Baldovan House
Balmuirfield
Playing Fields
School
Downfield Park
Downfield
Lawside Academy
Crematorium
Kirkton Park
Leisure Centre
Kingsway Campus Dundee College
KINGSWAY WEST RETAIL PARK
B&Q Superstore
DUNSINANE INDUSTRIAL ESTATE
Beechwood Park
Balfield Park
Fairmuir Park
Football Grnd
KINGS CROSS HOSP
WEST KINGSWAY
CLEPINGTON ROAD
A90
B960

E
F
G
H
1
2
3
4
5
6
8
15
16
Hilltown of Balmuir
Barns of Claverhouse Smallholdings
FORFAR ROAD
A90
EMMOCK ROAD
DUNTRUNE ROAD
South Powrie
Black Watch Memorial
Powrie Castle (remains)
Balmuir Farm
Claverhouse
EMMOCK WOODS DR
WOODS DR
FITZGERALD WAY
WILLIAM FITZGERALD WY
EMMOCK LA
CASTLEWOOD AV
MIDDLETON CRES
BARNS NEUK
EMMOCK WK
Barns of Claverhouse
CHARLES
JACK MARTIN WAY
CLAVERHOUSE EAST INDUSTRIAL ESTATE
CHEVIOT CRESCENT
GRAMPIAN
Playing Field
CLAVERHOUSE WEST INDUSTRIAL PARK
BOWMAN
Trottick
Mill Ponds
MANSION DRIVE
GRAHAM CT
GORDON CT
GILLESPIE TER
ORCHARD CT
DUFFUS CT
School
HERON RISE
TROTTICK MAINS
KILMORE TER
CLAVERHOUSE ROAD
CLAVERHOUSE OLD RD
BARNS OF CLAVERHOUSE RD
JOHN GRAHAME AV
SILVER BUTTON YD
ATHOLL YD
GLEN
HIGHLAND CHIEF WY
AVENUE
CHEVALIERS PEND
COVENANTERS PEND
VISCOUNTS PEND
FINDHORN STREET
FINDHORN PLACE
FINTRY DRIVE
FINELLA GDNS
FINELLA PLACE
FINELLA TER
FINDOWRIE ST
FINDHORN
FINDCASTLE ST
FINDCASTLE TER
FINDCASTLE PL
FINAVON STREET
FINAVON PLACE
FINAVON TERRACE
Liby
School
HEBRIDES DRIVE
GRUINARD TER
LEWIS TER
HARRIS TER
UIST TER
FOULA TER
COLONSAY TER
MULL TER
BARRA TER
LISMORE TER
ERISKAY DR
Park
Golf Course
Caird Park
Gelly Burn
GLAMIS ROAD
MAINS LOAN
Church (remains of)
Mains Castle
Club House
Stadium
Sports Ground
Playing Fields
FINTRY ROAD
FINTRY GDNS
FINEDON TER
FINTRY CRES
FINTRYSIDE
FINTRY RD
Fintry
Finlathen Park
FOUNTAINBLEAU DRIVE
AFTON PL
HONEYGREEN
CUMNOCK PL
DARVEL PL
PITKERRO DR
BALLOCHMYLE DR
GLENCONNER
LOMOND PL
RIDDELL TER
BLACKLOCK CRES
ROWANTREE CRES
MOSSGIEL PLACE
MOSSGIEL CRES
School
Playing Fields
Linlathen
R.F.C
ALLOWAY PL
ALLOWAY DRIVE
ALLOWAY TERRACE
JOAN BARTLETT HO
PRIORY CT
PITKERRO CT
MCMANUS CT
KINGENNIE CT
KERRYSTONE
CRAIGHILL
VALGREEN CT
LEYSHADE
PITKERRO ROAD
KINGSWAY
A929
A972
GRANTON TER
GRANTON PL
KERRSVIEW TERRACE
GRAHAM STREET
Sports Ground
AVENUE
WOODLANDS TERRACE
HAYWOOD PL
WOODSIDE TERRACE
WOODSIDE AV
MAINS DRIVE
MAINS TERRACE
Maryfield
Works
Dundee College
GRAHAM WYND
CARDROSS PL
LAMMERTON TERRACE
CASTLE TER
FORFAR RD
MARTIN STREET
NAIRN ST
MILNER ST
MACNABB ST
MACNABB PL
PITKERRO RD
CLEPINGTON ROAD
ARGYLE
DUFF ST
Maryfield

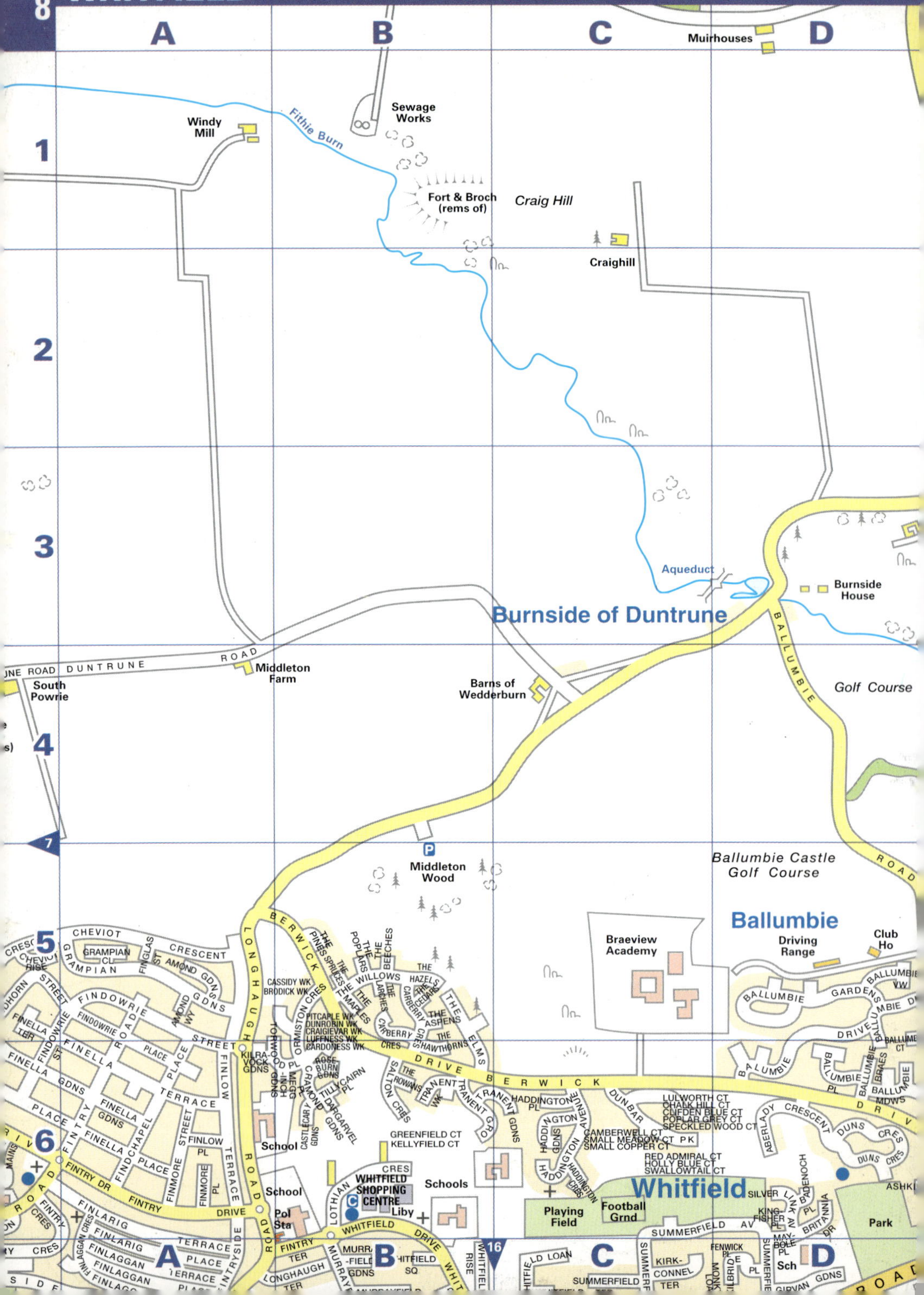

Muirhouses
Sewage Works
Windy Mill
Fithie Burn
Fort & Broch (rems of)
Craig Hill
Craighill
Aqueduct
Burnside House
Burnside of Duntrune
BALLUMBIE ROAD
Golf Course
DUNTRUNE ROAD
Middleton Farm
South Powrie
Barns of Wedderburn
Middleton Wood
Ballumbie Castle Golf Course
Ballumbie
Braeview Academy
Driving Range
Club Ho
CHEVIOT CRESCENT
GRAMPIAN CL
GRAMPIAN GDNS
FINDOWRIE STREET
FINLAGGAN PLACE
LONGHAUGH ROAD
BERWICK DRIVE
School
Schools
WHITFIELD SHOPPING CENTRE
Pol Sta
Liby
FINTRY DRIVE
WHITFIELD DRIVE
Playing Field
Football Grnd
Whitfield
SUMMERFIELD AV
Park
Sch

Kellas
Kellas Wood
Valgreen
West Mains of Gagie
Buckler Heads Wood
CHAPEL RD
BUCKLERS WYND
BUCKLERS CROFT
B978
Mill of Murroes
Rannoch Farm
Glack Hill
Duntrune Hill
Westhall Farm
Weir
Murroes
Murroes Castle
Murroes Burn
Ballumbie Castle (remains of)
Ballumbie House
Ballumbie Castle Golf Course
KELLAS ROAD
HAWTHORN GRO
POPLAR DR
CHESTNUT GRN
Fisher Burn
East Pitkerro
B961
DRUMSTURDY ROAD
Pikerro House
Rec Grnd
TRAQUAIR GDNS
THIRLESTANE PL
PEEBLES DRIVE
MACHRIE PL
CARRADALE DR
KINNARDALE PL
ARDMINISH PL
SUNADALE CT
OLD TOLL LOAN
CHIRNSIDE PL
MYRTLEHALL GDNS
SPARTLETON PL
SELKIRK GDNS
HAWICK DRIVE
BALLUMBIE
COLDSTREAM DR
MONTPELIER GDNS
DRUMGEITH ROAD
Works
FOWLER
WEST PITKERRO INDUSTRIAL ESTATE
10
17
E F G H
1 2 3 4 5 6

A
B
C
D
1
2
3
4
5
6
9
9
18
Woodside Wood
Buckler Heads Wood
Buddon Burn
Omachie Farm
St Bride's Ring Fort
Kingennie House
Kingennie
ROAD
SOUTH KINGENNIE STEADINGS
Viewbank Cottages
DRUMSTURDY
B961
Kincordie
Ethiebeaton
Gallow Hill
Ethiebeaton Quarry (Whinstone)
Cairn Greg
Quarry (dis)
Roman Hill
Leisure Club
Garden Centre
North Grange

Cunmont
SCHOOL RD
B962
ROAD
SANDERSON PL
Rec Grnd
Primary School
Newbigging
PITAIRLIE
Downieken
DRUMSTURDY ROAD
LAWS COTTAGES
Drumsturdy
Downie Mill
Laws
Fort & Broch
Laws Hill
A92
Souterrain
Ardownie Quarry
ROAD
Ardownie
ARBROATH
Motel
VICTORIA
St Kanes Well
Ashludie Farm
STREET
B962
BROOMHILL DR
PARK VW
Rec Grnd
Ardestie Links
E
F
G
H
1
2
3
4
5
6

A
B
C
D
1
2
3
4
5
6
Gray House
Charlestown
WESTER GOURDIE IND EST
NCR Discovery Centre
Denhead of Gray
New Mill of Gray
Lochee Burn
KINGSWAY
Stone Circle (rems of)
Lynch Sports Centre
South Road Park
Motel
Fowlis Burn
Offices
Swallow Hotel
DUNDEE TECHNOLOGY PARK
Health Centre
DUNDEE MEDIPARK
Carseview Centre
A90
PERTH ROAD
RIVERSIDE AVENUE
Invergowrie Burn
DELTA CENTRE
School
Invergowrie
Scottish Crop Research Intitute
Memorial Park
INVERGOWRIE
Old Quarry Wildlife Centre
Kingoodie Quarries (disused)
Pier (dis)
Pier
ERROL ROAD
RIVERSIDE
MAIN STREET
GREYSTANE ROAD
SOUTH ROAD
EXPLORER ROAD
MYREKIRK ROAD
FULTON ROAD
WADE STREET
BRUNEL RD
ARROL RD
NOBEL RD
STATION ROAD
MARINER DRIVE
CHARLESTON DRIVE

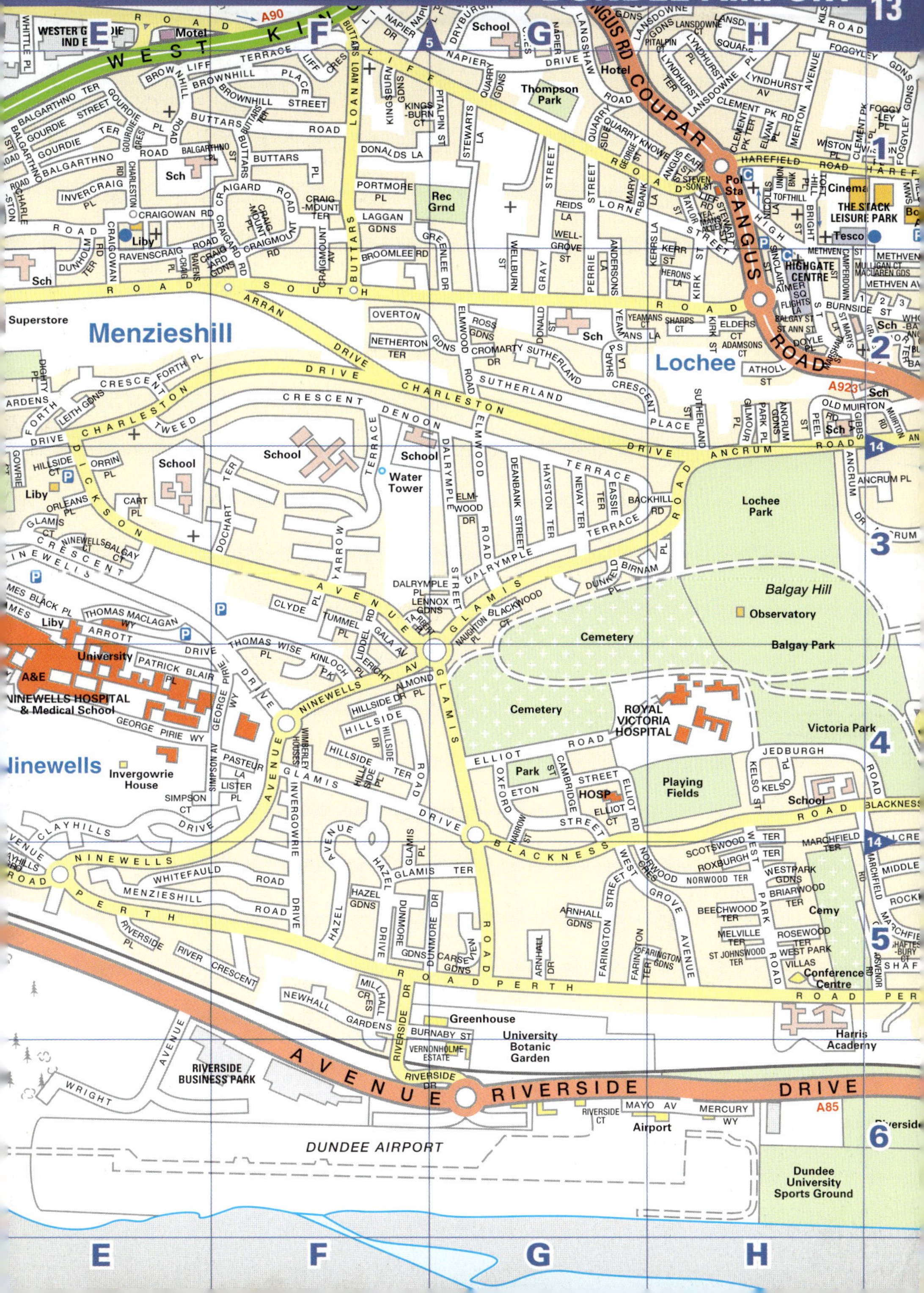
E
F
G
H
1
2
3
4
5
6
A90
A923
A85
5
14
WEST KINGSWAY
COUPAR ANGUS RD
Motel
Hotel
School
Thompson Park
Rec Grnd
Pol Sta
Cinema
THE STACK LEISURE PARK
Tesco
HIGHGATE CENTRE
Superstore
Menzieshill
Lochee
Sch
Liby
Water Tower
Lochee Park
Balgay Hill
Observatory
Balgay Park
Cemetery
University
A&E
NINEWELLS HOSPITAL & Medical School
Ninewells
Invergowrie House
ROYAL VICTORIA HOSPITAL
Victoria Park
Park
HOSP
Playing Fields
Cemy
Conference Centre
Greenhouse
University Botanic Garden
Harris Academy
RIVERSIDE BUSINESS PARK
Airport
DUNDEE AIRPORT
Dundee University Sports Ground
SOUTH ROAD
ARRAN DRIVE
CHARLESTON DRIVE
DICKSON AVENUE
GLAMIS ROAD
NINEWELLS AVENUE
PERTH ROAD
BLACKNESS ROAD
ELLIOT ROAD
RIVERSIDE AVENUE
RIVERSIDE DRIVE
ANCRUM ROAD
LOCHEE ROAD
MENZIESHILL ROAD
CLAYHILLS DRIVE

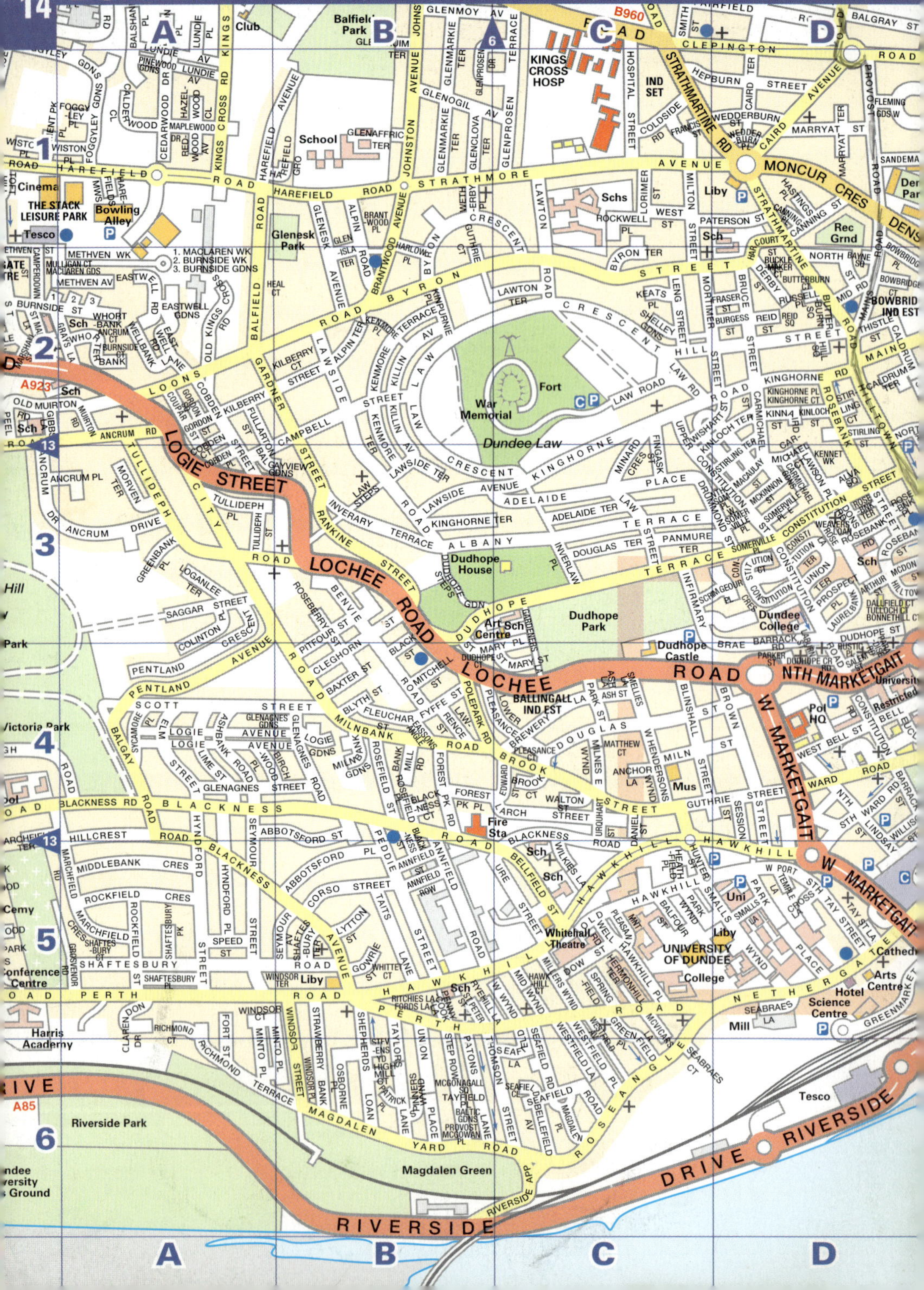

A
B
C
D
1
2
3
4
5
6
B960
6
13
A923
A85
Club
Balfield Park
GLENMOY AV
KINGS CROSS HOSP
IND SET
CLEPINGTON ROAD
BALGRAY ST
STRATHMARTINE RD
HEPBURN STREET
WEDDERBURN
MARRYAT TER
PROVOST RD
FLEMING GDNS W
SANDEMAN
MONCUR CRES
Liby
Schs
ROCKWELL PL
PATERSON ST
Sch
Rec Grnd
NORTH BAYNE
BOWBRIDGE
BOWBRIDGE IND EST
School
GLENAFFRIC TER
STRATHMORE AVENUE
HAREFIELD ROAD
Cinema
THE STACK LEISURE PARK
Bowling Alley
Tesco
Glenesk Park
1. MACLAREN WK
2. BURNSIDE WK
3. BURNSIDE GDNS
METHVEN WK
METHVEN AV
EASTWELL RD
BYRON STREET
LAWTON TER
LAW CRESCENT
KINGHORNE RD
HILLTOWN
MAIN ST
Fort
War Memorial
Dundee Law
LAW ROAD
LOONS ROAD
KILBERRY ST
CAMPBELL ST
LOGIE STREET
LOCHEE ROAD
ANCRUM RD
TULLIDEPH PL
ANCRUM DRIVE
ALBANY TERRACE
ADELAIDE PLACE
INVERARY TERRACE
KINGHORNE TER
Dudhope House
Dudhope Park
DUDHOPE TERRACE
CONSTITUTION ROAD
SOMERVILLE PL
Dundee College
Dudhope Castle
Art Centre
SAGGAR STREET
COLINTON PL
PENTLAND AVENUE
PENTLAND CRES
Hill
Park
Victoria Park
SCOTT STREET
LOGIE AVENUE
GLENAGNES ROAD
MILNBANK ROAD
BALLINGALL IND EST
DOUGLAS STREET
BROOK STREET
ANCHOR LA
Mus
NTH MARKETGAIT
W MARKETGAIT
Pol HQ
WEST BELL ST
WARD ROAD
University
BLACKNESS RD
BLACKNESS ROAD
BLACKNESS AVENUE
HILLCREST ROAD
ABBOTSFORD ST
Fire Sta
WALTON ST
HAWKHILL
MIDDLEBANK CRES
ROCKFIELD CRES
SHAFTESBURY ROAD
Cemy
Conference Centre
Uni
UNIVERSITY OF DUNDEE
Whitehall Theatre
College
PERTH ROAD
NETHERGATE
Hotel
Science Centre
Arts Centre
Cathedral
Mill
Harris Academy
RICHMOND TERRACE
MAGDALEN YARD ROAD
SEABRAES LA
Tesco
RIVERSIDE DRIVE
Riverside Park
Magdalen Green
RIVERSIDE APP
Dundee University Ground

E
F
G
H
1
2
3
4
5
6
16
Dundee College
Maryfield House
Sports Complex
Park
College
Academy
Craigie Park
TA Centre
Baxter Park
Rec Grnd
Mayfield Rec Grnd
Tannadice Park
Hilltown
School
Works
Pol Sta
Sch
Liby
WELLGATE SHOPPING CENTRE
Bus Sta
THE FORUM
Mus
T.H
EAST DOCK RD RETAIL PARK
Camperdown Dock
Victoria Dock
Frigate Unicorn
SHOPPING CENTRE
North Carr Lightship
Hotel
Toll
Queen Elizabeth Wharf
King George V Wharf
Caledon West Wharf
Princes Alexandra Wharf
Eastern Wharf
Dundee Harbour
Fowler Rock
Beacon Rock
Olympia Leisure Centre
RSS Discovery
Discovery Point
DUNDEE
FIRTH OF TAY
TAY ROAD BRIDGE
A92
A972
B959
CLEPINGTON ROAD
FORFAR ROAD
ALBERT ST
ARBROATH ROAD
VICTORIA ROAD
KING ST
PRINCES ST
SEAGATE
EAST DOCK STREET
MARKETGAIT
SOUTH MARKETGAIT
DENS ROAD
LYON ST
PITKERRO ROAD
DURA STREET
BROUGHTY FERRY ROAD
CRAIGIE ROAD
DALKEITH ROAD
MAINS LOAN
STRATHMORE ST
DUNDONALD STREET
ARKLAY STREET
CAMPERDOWN STREET
MARINE PARADE
DOCK STREET
DISCOVERY QUAY
EARL GREY PL
COWGATE
MEADOWSIDE
MURRAYGATE
CASTLE ST
HIGH ST
CITY SQ
CRICHTON ST
UNION ST
1. TANNADICE CT
2. CLEPINGTON CT
3. DUNDONALD CT

A
B
C
D
1
2
3
4
5
6
8
7
15
Pol Sta
Playing Field
Football Grnd
Park
Sch
School
Quarry (dis)
Playing Field
Drumgeith Park
Supermarket
SHOPPING CENTRE
Bingo
Fitness Centre
LONGTOWN IND EST
Cinema
Wks
ASDA
B&Q
RETAIL PARK
Fire Sta
MID CRAIGIE INDUSTRIAL ESTATE
Craigie
Eastern Cemetery
Douglas & Angus
Rec Grnd
Monymusk Park
Gardyne Campus
Physical Education College
Works
Stannergate
Tidal Harbour
Caledon East Wharf
Prince Charles Wharf
Eastern Wharf
FIRTH OF
KINGSWAY EAST
A972
B959
A92
ARBROATH ROAD
BROUGHTY FERRY ROAD
DUNDEE ROAD
WEST DUNDEE
DRUMGEITH ROAD
DOUGLAS ROAD
GREENDYKES ROAD
HAPPYHILLOCK ROAD
PITKERRO ROAD
BALUNIE DRIVE
BALUNIE AVENUE
BALLINDEAN ROAD
LONGTOWN ROAD
MID CRAIGIE ROAD
CRAIGIE DRIVE
STANNERGATE
STRIPS OF CRAIGIE ROAD
WHITFIELD DRIVE
WHITFIELD AVENUE
SUMMERFIELD AV
PIPER STREET
FINDALE STREET
FINTRYSIDE
FINLARIG TERRACE
FINLARIG PLACE
FINLAGGAN TERRACE
FINLAGGAN PLACE
FINLAGGAN CRES
FOUNTAINBLEAU DR
MIDMILL ROAD
DRUMLANRIG DRIVE
BALLANTRAE PLACE
BALMORAL TERRACE
BALERNO STREET
BALBEGGIE
ABOYNE AVENUE
HUNTLY ROAD
GOTTERSTONE
SEAFORTH
DAWSON ROAD
STRATHERN ROAD
ALBANY
BRINGTON
SOUTHAMPTON PL
CRAIGIE AVENUE
CROMBIE TER
NORAN AVENUE
MURRAY ST
HARBOUR VIEW
CAROLINA CT
FISH DOCK RD
MARGARET CRES
LAVENDER ST

E
F
G
H
1
2
3
4
5
6
DRUMGEITH ROAD
B961
BALDOVIE ROAD
Works
BALDOVIE INDUSTRIAL ESTATE
WEST PITKERRO INDUSTRIAL ESTATE
FOWLER RD
MUIRHEAD PL
BARLOW AVENUE
BAKER STREET
IVORY PL
AINSLIE AVENUE
PEARCE
BERYL ST
Linlathen
BALUNIEFIELD TRADING ESTATE
Dighty Water
BALUNIE DRIVE
BROUGHTY FERRY WALK
BROUGHTY FERRY CT
Supermarket
JOHNSTONE
INDUSTRIAL ESTATE
Lilac Cottage
BALMORAL GDNS
BALUNIE STREET
BALUNIE AVENUE
BALUNIE TERRACE
BALLATER PL
BALUNIEFIELD RD
Whitton Pk Football Grnd
Sports Centre
Claypotts Park
School
ARBROATH ROAD
ROSSIE AVENUE
BALGILLO RD
BOYSACK
Rec Grnd
Castle
CLAYPOTTS CASTLE GDNS
CLAYPOTTS RD
Dawson Park
West Ferry
Garden
CAMPERDOWN
Sports Centre
Playing Fields
School
STRATHERN ROAD
NORTHWOOD CT
Hotel
SEAFIELD TER
NURSERY ROAD
Fort Hill
Taychreggan Hotel
Grove Academy
Acad
Yacht Club
WEST QUEEN STREET
QUEEN STREET
Health Centre
Liby
BROUGHTY FERRY
DUNDEE ROAD
BROOK STREET
KING STREET
FISHER STREET
GRAY STREET
BEACH CRES
Lifeboat Station
Pier
Castle Green
Broughty Castle
Harbour
Broughty Rock
Broughty Ferry
TAY
18
9

A
B
C
D
10
Roman Hill
North Grange
Balmossie Farm
1
2
3
4
5
6
Linlathen
Balmossie Bridge
ARBROATH ROAD
A92
Hotel
SHOPPING CENTRE
Tennis Club
Dighty Water
Viaduct
School
Playing Field
Barnhill
Barnhill Cemy
Fire Sta
SHOPPING CENTRE
Hotel
Hall
BALMOSSIE
FERRY ROAD
DALHOUSIE ROAD
MONIFIETH ROAD
A930
Reres Hill
Barnhill Rock Garden
Playing Fields
Black Rocks
Orchar Park
Groynes
Mussel Beds
ESPLANADE
17

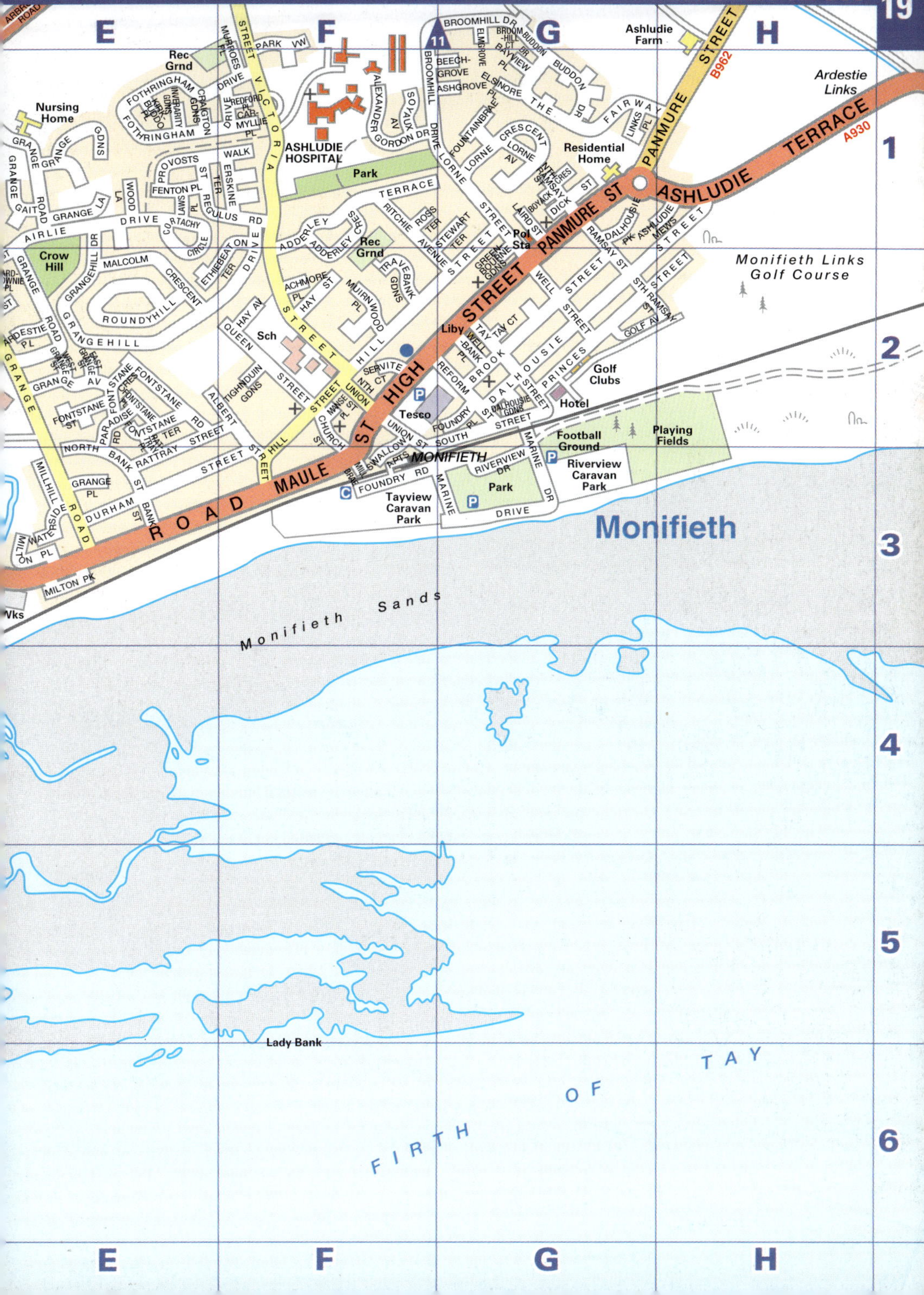
E
F
G
H
1
2
3
4
5
6
Ashludie Farm
Ardestie Links
Nursing Home
Rec Grnd
ASHLUDIE HOSPITAL
Park
Residential Home
ASHLUDIE TERRACE
A930
PANMURE STREET
B962
PANMURE ST
HIGH STREET
MAULE ST
ROAD
Crow Hill
Rec Grnd
Pol Sta
Monifieth Links Golf Course
Sch
Liby
Tesco
Golf Clubs
Hotel
Football Ground
Playing Fields
MONIFIETH
Riverview Caravan Park
Tayview Caravan Park
Park
Monifieth
Monifieth Sands
Lady Bank
FIRTH OF TAY
Wks

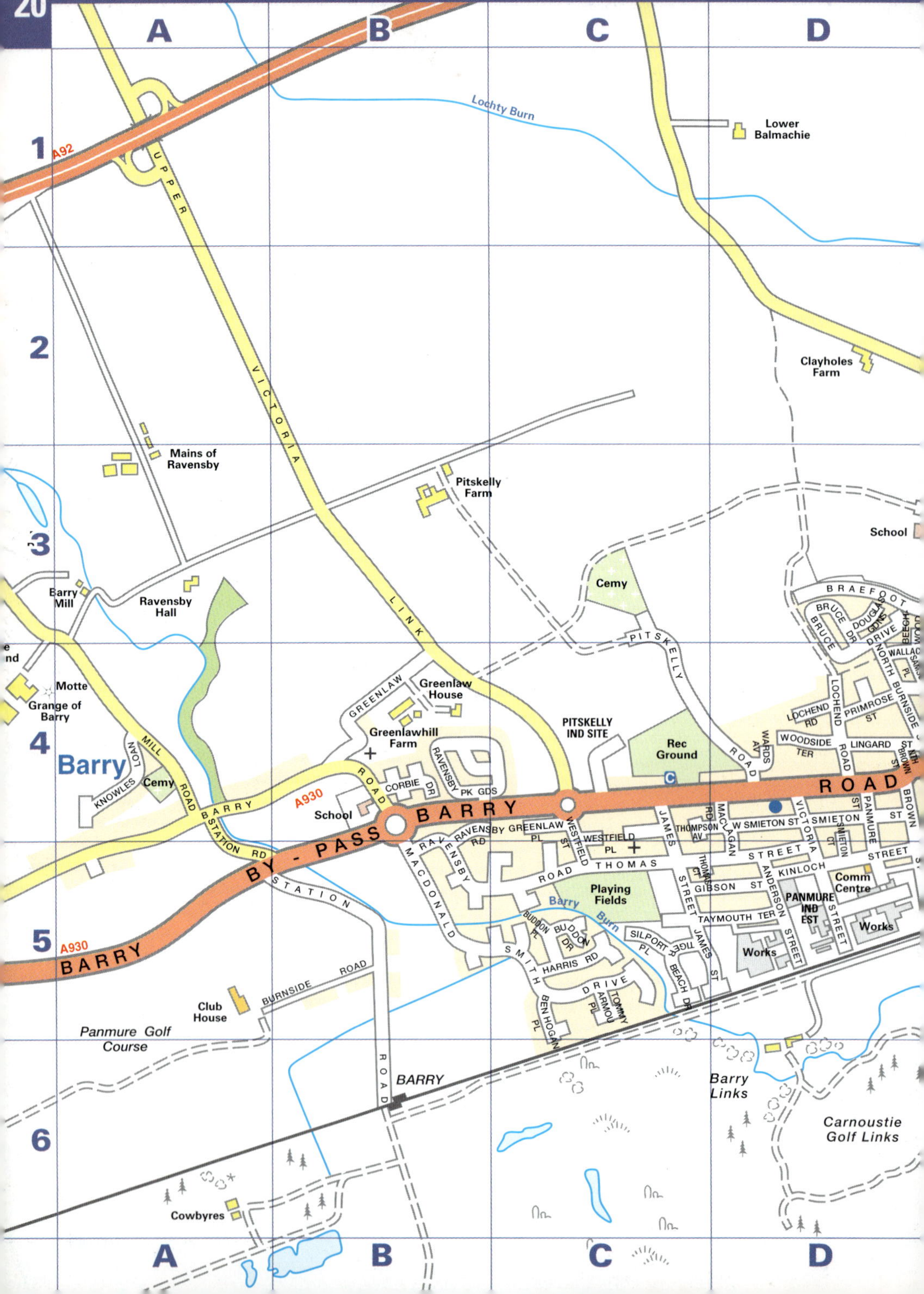
A
B
C
D
1
2
3
4
5
6
A92
Lochty Burn
Lower Balmachie
UPPER VICTORIA LINK
Clayholes Farm
Mains of Ravensby
Pitskelly Farm
School
Cemy
Barry Mill
Ravensby Hall
PITSKELLY ROAD
BRAEFOOT
Motte
Grange of Barry
Greenlaw House
GREENLAW
Greenlawhill Farm
PITSKELLY IND SITE
Rec Ground
Barry
KNOWLES LOAN
MILL ROAD
Cemy
BARRY ROAD
A930
School
CORBIE DR
RAVENSBY PK GDS
BARRY BY - PASS
ROAD
STATION RD
STATION ROAD
MACDONALD
RAVENSBY RD
GREENLAW PL
WESTFIELD ST
WESTFIELD PL
THOMAS ROAD
JAMES STREET
THOMPSON AV
MACLAGAN ST
W SMIETON ST
VICTORIA ST
SMIETON ST
PANMURE ST
BROWN ST
KINLOCH
ANDERSON STREET
GIBSON ST
TAYMOUTH TER
PANMURE IND EST
PANMURE STREET
Comm Centre
Works
Playing Fields
Barry Burn
BUDDON PL
BUDDON DR
SMITH
HARRIS RD
SILPORT PL
BEACH DR
DRIVE
TOMMY ARMOUR PL
BEN HOGAN PL
LOCHEND RD
LOCHEND ROAD
PRIMROSE ST
LINGARD ST
WOODSIDE TER
WARDS AV
NORTH BURNSIDE ST
WALLACE PL
DOUGLAS GDNS
BRUCE DR
BRUCE DRIVE
A930
BARRY
BURNSIDE ROAD
Club House
Panmure Golf Course
BARRY
Barry Links
Carnoustie Golf Links
Cowbyres

E
F
G
H
1
2
3
4
5
6
A930
Carlogie Farm
Carlogie House Hotel
CARLOGIE RD
CARLOGIE ROAD
Craigmill Burn
Hall
Primary School
The Old Manor
Panbride
Lochty Burn
PANBRIDE ROAD
WESTHAVEN ROAD
MANOR GDNS
PANBRIDE VW
CHAPMAN DRIVE
CRAIGMILL GDNS
Recreation Ground
DOBSON DRIVE
NICHOLL PL
NEWTON ROAD
NEWTON CRES
NEWTON CRESCENT
Sch
SPENCER CRES
CAESAR AV
CAESAR AVENUE
Rec Grnd
LINEFIELD ROAD
West Haven
HANWELL RD
BRAEHEAD DRIVE
BALMACHIE ROAD
Woodlands Caravan Park
QUEEN STREET
HOLYROOD
ELIZABETH CRES
KEITH AV
TENNIS ROAD
CONDOR CT
MACKENZIE ST
DALHOUSIE
KIRK WK
LEYSMILL CL
WESTHAVEN PK
CRAIG PL
LOMOND DR
LOWNIE RD
BROADLANDS
WATERSIDE
EAST ROW VW
Carnoustie Park
BRAEFOOT
WOODLEA GDNS
JARVIS PL
YEAMAN STREET
MILLAR STREET
MAULE STREET
GUTHRIE ST
PANBRIDE PL
PANBRIDE ST
LOWSON ST
McGILL PL
WINTER PL
Bowling Grn
GREEN LA
LOCHTY STREET
WILLIAM PL
WILLIAMSTON PL
EARL
ARBROATH STREET
ROSE STREET
ROCK ST
THISTLE ST
WEST PATH
TERRACE
KIRKTON TER
COLLIER ROAD
PHILIP STREET
CHURCH ST
Pol Sta
Council Offices
CAMUS CT
SIMPSON PL
BALFOUR PL
DUNDEE STREET
HIGH STREET
IRELAND STREET
LONG ROW
NORRIES RD
MARINER ST
ADMIRAL ST
SEABRAE
Harbour
Liby
STATION RD
FOX ST
BONELLA ST
CARNOUSTIE
TAYSIDE PARADE
BURNSIDE GDNS
BURNSIDE
CAMUS ST
MAYFIELD LA
Sch
LINKS
Hall
Health Cen
FERRIER STREET
PARK AV
LOUSEN PK
Fire Sta
RUXTON PL
KINLOCH PK
KINLOCH STREET
GOLF ST
STH KINLOCH ST
TAYMOUTH AV
BRUCE CT
LINKS PARADE
Leisure Centre
Club
PARK HOMES
CHARLES ST
GOLF ST
TAYMOUTH STREET
SOUTH TAYMOUTH ST
LINKS
Carnoustie Golf Course Hotel
Carnoustie
The Brithers
Burnside Golf Course
Championship Golf Course
Club House
Buddon Links Golf Course
Carnoustie Bay
Barry Sands

A
B
C
D
1
2
3
4
5
6
Middle Bank
FIRTH OF TAY
Tay Bridge
Cows Hole
Pier
RANKINE CT
ST FORT ROAD
BEACH RD
RIVERSIDE GDNS
ROAD
School
ST FORT PL
MARS GDNS
WOODHAVEN TER
WEST ACRES DR
WOODHAVEN AV
WESTWATER PL
NORTH TER
FLASS RD
FLASS
ERICHT RD
AVENUE
HIGHFIELD AV
TERRACE
RIVERSIDE
SCOTS WOOD CRES
BIRKHILL AV
CROSSHILL
Woodhaven
Wormit Bay
Long Craig
Lifeboat Sta
ROAD
Hall
BRIDGEHEAD PL
HILLPARK RD
NORTHVIEW TER
TERRACE
HILL CRES
RESERVOIR RD
MT STEWART RD
HILL PARK
Wormit Hill
STRATHBLAIR AV
GLEN LEVEN DR
CRAIGSHANNOCH
BAY RD
DEVONLEA RD
VIEWMOUNT RD
Wormit
NAUGHTON
B946
Wormit Farm
P

Newport-on-Tay
Craig Head
Sea Craig
Eel Craig
Jetty
Pluck the Crow Point
Tayfield House
Servite House
Curling Pond
Park
Tennis Club
Gowrie Hill
Liby
Surgery
School
Forgan Arts Centre
Tofts Law
Inverdovat Farm
INVERDOVAT LANE
Sports Centre
Playing Fields
Muttonhole Wood
St Fort Hill
North Hill
Roseberry Wood
Dovecot
St Fort Home Farm
Pond Cottage
Wester Friarton
Farm Cottages
Pol Sta
HOSP
WATERSON CROOK
TAY ROAD BRIDGE
A92
B946
A914
TAYPORT RD
TAY STREET
HIGH ST
HIGH ROAD
WEST ROAD
BOAT BRAE
BOAT ROAD
CUPAR ROAD
KIRK ROAD
JAMES ST
ROBERT ST
WILLIAM ST
GOWRIE ST
KERR STREET
BANK ST
TAY TERRACE
EAST QUEEN ST
PROSPECT TER
TAYVIEW TER
NORTHFIELD RD
ELIZABETH CRES
CRAIGHEAD RD
CRAIGHEAD CRES
NORWOOD
WHINFIELD PL
NORWOOD LA
SYLVAN LA
KILGASK ST
STATION PL
STATION BRAE
STRUAN ST
STRUAN PL
MYRTLE TER
DALE PL
YOUNGSTREET
ALBERT CRES
LINDEN AVENUE
VICTORIA ST
KILNBURN
UNION PL
UNION ST
KING ST
QUEEN ST
WOODBINE TER
SEACRAIG CT
BLYTH ST
BLYTH CT
SCOTT ST
GRANARY LA
SCOTSCRAIG
KINBRAE PK
KINBRAE PK GDNS
KINBRAE CT
SHEPHERDS RD
SHEPHERDS BRAE
WOODMUIR CRES
WOODMUIR PL
RIVERSIDE LA
WELLGATE
WELL PK
BEECHWOOD TER WEST
BEECHWOOD TER EAST
BRIDGE ST
FORGAN ST
FORGAN WY
WESTWOOD TER
CASTLE BRAE
CASTLE BANK
WESTFIELD TER
ALMA TER
NETHERLEA PL
WESTPARK RD
E
F
G
H
1
2
3
4
5
6

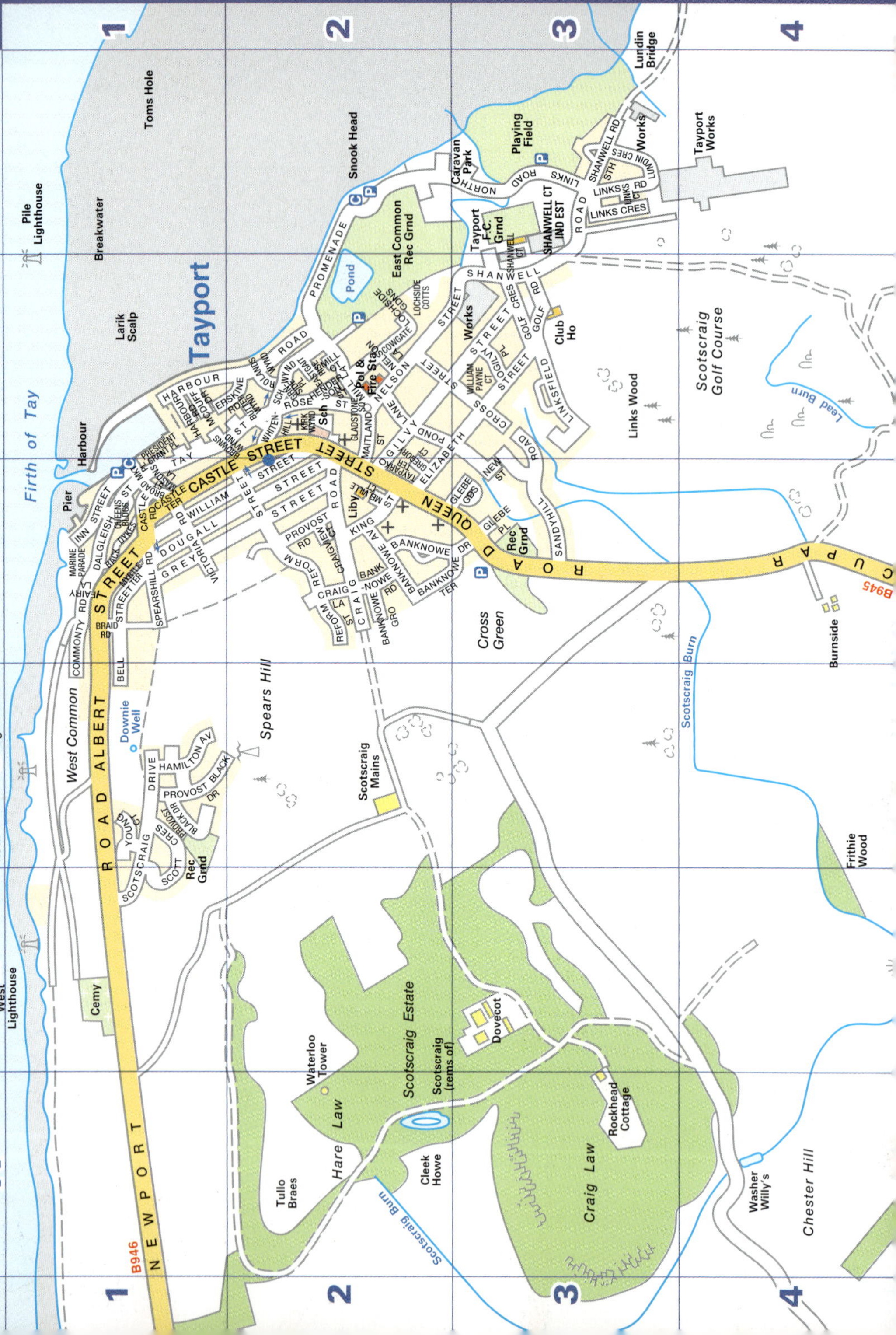
Firth of Tay
Tayport
Harbour
Pier
Breakwater
Pile Lighthouse
Larik Scalp
Toms Hole
Snook Head
East Lighthouse
West Lighthouse
Cradle Rock
West Common
Cemy
NEWPORT ROAD
ALBERT STREET
CASTLE STREET
QUEEN STREET
CUPAR ROAD
B946
B945
Spears Hill
Scotscraig Mains
Scotscraig Estate
Scotscraig (rems of)
Dovecot
Waterloo Tower
Hare Law
Tullo Braes
Cleek Howe
Craig Law
Rockhead Cottage
Washer Willy's
Chester Hill
Frithie Wood
Burnside
Cross Green
Scotscraig Burn
Scotscraig Golf Course
Links Wood
Lead Burn
Club Ho
Tayport Works
Lundin Bridge
Playing Field
Caravan Park
Tayport F.C. Grnd
East Common Rec Grnd
Pond
Pol & Fire Stn
Downie Well
Rec Grnd
SHANWELL CT IND EST

Cupar
Upper Dalgairn
Cupar Muir
Cupar Golf Course
River Eden
Owlet Wood
Tarvit Farm
Balass Den
Tarvit Cottages
Tailabout
Sewage Works
CUPAR TRADING ESTATE
EDEN VALLEY BUSINESS PARK
ADAMSON HOSPITAL
Howe of Fife R.F. Grnd
Duffus Park
Douglas Bader Garden
Bowls & Cricket Grnd
Cupar Sports Centre
Elmwood College
School
Ferrymuir
Mayfield
Club House
Cemy
Fire Sta
Tesco
Works
Park
T.H & Council Bldgs
GRANARY BUSINESS CENTRE
EAST ROAD
SOUTH ROAD
WEST PORT
BONNYGATE
CARSLOGIE ROAD
BALGARVIE ROAD
PITSCOTTIE ROAD
CERES ROAD
BRIGHTON ROAD
WESTFIELD ROAD
DRUM ROAD
A91
A913
A916
B940

Balmullo
Leuchars
St Michaels
A914
A919
B945
MAIN STREET
SCHOOL ROAD
CLAY ROAD
LUCKLAW RD
QUARRY ROAD
SMITHY LA
MCWALTERS FIELDS
MANSFIELD RD
HAYSTON
LOMOND PL
MURRAY ROW
MURRAY CT
SMITHY RD
PARK
STRAITON TER
CYNICUS PL
DRIVE
Surgery
Balmullo Farm
BURNSIDE
BORTHWICK PL
PITCAIRN
PITCAIRN DR
ANDERSON DR
INCHLAW
Burnside Hall
DUNEDIN PK
PARK VIEW
HILLFIELD RD
SUMMER-HILL
GREEN ACRE
HILLVIEW ROAD
THE MOUNT
DAVID WILSON PK
Sch
Rec Grnd
Cycle-Cross Racing Track
Comerton
Earlshall
Dovecot
EARLSHALL ROAD
BEAUFORT CRES
BEAUFORT CL
CRESCENT
HUNTER CRES
HAMPDEN CL
WARWICK CL
PITLETHIE ROAD
HENDERSON TER
SCHOOL HILL
SCHOOL BRAE
MAIN STREET
ADAM CL
BAKER PL
ESSEX
NICHOLLS
WESSEX AV
FREEMAN GRO
AVENUE DRIVE
PLAYFAIR
TUTTLE CL
TUTOR CL
TUTOR ROAD
HUDSON PL
KEITH CRES
SERVITE CT
THE CROFT
REDCROFT PL
ROSS RD
INNES RD
NORMAN VW
MEARS CT
PITCAIRN PK
RAF LEUCHARS
JAVELIN CRES
BLENHEIM PL
SPITFIRE PL
WHIRLWIND PL
Playing Field
FERN PL
MEADOW RD
ST BUNYANS PL
AITKEN PL
Rosebank Park Homes
Leuchars Castle
Castleknowe Motte
Dovecot
Cemy
Club House
War Memorial
St Michaels Wood
The White House
St Michaels Golf Course
Gallow Hill
Hotel
Angus Cottage
Motray Water
Pusk Wood
1
2
3
4
A
B
C
D
E
F

Guardbridge
LEUCHARS AIRFIELD
RAF LEUCHARS
Wind Gauge
Coble House Point
Coble Shore
River Eden
Bird Observatory
OLD ST ANDREWS RD
Guard Bridge
Paper Mill
Inner Bridge
MAIN STREET
KINNEAR CT
MCGREGORS BUILDINGS
Primary School
INNERBRIDGE ST
RIVER TER
MOTRAY PK
Rec Grnd
MILTONBANK CRES
MOTRAY CRES
TOLL ROAD
STATION ROAD
LEUCHARS
ANSON WK
ROW
METEOR PL
Reservoir
Milton
Moonzie Burn
Seggie Farm Cottages
Seggie
CUPAR ROAD
A91
Pusk
Farm Cottages
Pusk Farm

A
B
C
D
1
2
3
4
5
6
A91
Balgrove Links
Strathtyrum Course
The Old Course
The New Course
Jubilee Course
Pilmour House
Club House
Driving Range
Strathtyrum Farm
Strathtyrum House
Dovecot (restored)
Balgove
GUARDBRIDGE ROAD
St Andrews Links Club House
Old Course Hotel
Club House
Playing Field
Madras College Rugby Club
North Haugh
ST ANDREWS UNIVERSITY
Hall
New Hall
Science Building
Physical Education & Sports Centre
University Playing Fields
Observatory
Northbank Farm
STRATHKINNESS HIGH ROAD
Conference Centre
David Russell Halls
FIFE PARK
WEST ACRES
B939
STRATHKINNESS LOW ROAD
BUCHANAN GARDENS
HEPBURN GARDENS
Cemy
Carron Lodge
School
Sch
Carron Bridge
LITTLE CARRON GDNS
YOUNGER GDS
Hallow Hill
Kinnes Burn
LADE BRAES
TRINITY PL
HALLOW HILL
PRIORY GDS
LAMOND DRIVE
KNOX ROAD
JOHN KNOX ROAD
WINDSOR GARDENS
AIKMAN PL
INDUSTRIAL ESTATE
BOBBY JONES PL
Balone
Craigtoun Meadows Holiday Park
Lumbo Den
Cairns Den
Cairnsmill Burn
LOVERS LANE
A915
LARGO

E
F
G
H
1
2
3
4
5
6
West Sands
St Andrews Bay
Long Rocks
Dunes
SANDS ROAD
BRUCE EMBANKMENT
Step Rock
Aquarium
Golf Mus
Royal & Ancient Club Ho
GRANNIE CLARKS WYND
THE LINKS
GIBSON PL
PILMOUR LINKS
John Burnet Hall
University Liby
Cinema
Castle & Visitor Centre
ST ANDREWS
St Salvators College
NORTH ST
SCORES
EAST SCORES
CITY ROAD
Bus Sta
Kinburn Park
Museum
MARKET STREET
Offices
Pol Sta
Liby
Mus
Cathedral
Piers
SOUTH STREET
T.H
Theatre
THE PENDS
Mill Port
Burn Stools
ARGYLE ST
DOUBLE DYKES RD
School
Schools
Abbey Wall
ABBEY WALK
ABBEY ST
St Marys College
Madras College
St Regulus Hall
QUEENS TER
Cockshaugh Park
BASSAGUARD IND EST
BRIDGE ST
St Andrews Botanic Gardens
THE CANONGATE
CANONGATE
School
HOSP
East Sands
Kinness Burn
Woodburn Park
ST MARY ST
St Davids Resource Centre
University Laboratory
Maidens Rock
AULD BURN RD
Rec Grnd
Football Grnd
ST NICHOLAS ST
LAMOND DRIVE
East Sands Leisure Centre
Fire Sta
IND EST
Health Centre
Playing Field
School & Nursery
Madras College
Nursery School
Kinkells Braes Caravan Park
ANSTRUTHER ROAD
A917
LARGO ROAD
STONEHO. BUSINESS CEN.
Amb Sta
KILRYMONT ROAD
Supermarket
Pipeland Farm
LAMBERTON PLACE

A - Z INDEX TO STREETS

with Postcodes

The Index includes some names for which there is insufficient space on the maps. These names are indicated by an * and are followed by the nearest adjoining thoroughfare.

Abbey Ct KY16 29 F3
Abbey St KY16 29 F3
Abbey Walk KY16 29 G4
Abbotsford Cres KY16 29 E3
Abbotsford Pl, Dundee DD2 14 B5
Abbotsford Pl, St Andrews KY16 29 E3
Abbotsford St DD2 14 A4
Abercorn St DD4 15 H1
Abercromby St DD5 18 B3
Aberdour Pl DD5 18 B3
Aberfoyle Gdns DD5 17 H3
Aberlady Cres DD4 8 D6
Abernethy Rd DD5 18 B3
Abertay Cres DD5 18 B4
Abertay Gdns DD5 18 C4
Abertay St DD5 18 B4
Aboyne Av DD4 16 C3
Academy Ter*, Forfar Rd DD4 15 F2
Accordion Way DD2 4 B2
Achmore Pl DD5 19 F2
Adam Cl KY16 26 E4
Adamson Ct KY15 25 C1
Adamsons Ct DD2 13 H2
Adderley Cres DD5 19 F1
Adderley Ter DD5 19 F2
Addison Rd DD5 18 A4
Adelaide Pl DD3 14 C3
Adelaide Ter DD3 14 C3
Admiral St DD7 21 H4
Afton Pl DD4 7 G5
Agnes Sq DD5 18 A6
Aikman Pl KY16 28 C6
Aimer Sq DD2 13 H2
Ainslie St DD5 17 F2
Airlie Dr DD5 19 E1
Airlie Pl DD1 3 A4
Aitken Pl KY16 26 C4
Albany Dr DD5 17 E4
Albany Gro DD5 16 D4
Albany Pk, Dundee DD5 17 E4
Albany Pk, St Andrews KY16 29 G4
Albany Pl, Dundee DD5 16 D5
Albany Pl, St Andrews KY16 29 E3
Albany Rd DD5 16 D5
Albany Ter DD3 14 B3
Albert Cres DD6 23 G2
Albert Gdns DD5 17 G5
Albert Rd DD5 17 F5
Albert Sq DD1 3 D2
Albert St, Dundee DD4 15 F2
Albert St, Monifieth DD5 19 E2
Albert St, Tayport DD6 24 C1
Alder Av DD5 18 D1
Alder Dr DD5 18 D1
Alder Pl DD5 18 D1
Alex Paterson La KY16 28 B5
Alexander Gordon Dr DD5 19 F1
Alexander St DD3 15 E3
Alexandra Ct KY16 29 E3
Alexandra Pl KY16 29 E3
Alford Gdns DD5 16 D3
Alfred Pl KY16 29 E3
Alison Pl KY16 29 F4
Alistair Soutar Cres DD2 12 B4
Allan La DD1 3 E2
Allan Robertson Dr KY16 29 F6
Alloway Halls DD4 7 G6
Alloway Pl DD4 7 G6
Alloway Pl West DD4 7 G6
Alloway Ter DD4 7 H6
Alma Ter DD6 23 E4
Almond Pl DD2 13 F4
Alpin Rd DD3 14 B1
Alpin Ter DD3 14 B2
Alva Sq DD3 14 D3
Ambleside Av DD3 6 D4
Ambleside Gdns DD3 6 D4
Ambleside Gro DD3 6 D4
Ambleside Ter DD3 6 D4
Ambrose St DD5 17 H6
Americanmuir Rd DD3 6 A4
Amond Gdns DD4 8 A5
Amond Way DD4 8 A5
Ancrum Ct DD2 14 A2
Ancrum Dr DD2 13 H3
Ancrum Gdns DD2 13 H2
Ancrum Pl DD2 13 H3
Ancrum Rd DD2 13 H3
Anderson Dr KY16 26 E2
Anderson St DD7 20 D5
Andersons La DD2 13 G1
Andrew Lang Cres KY16 28 B5
Andrew Thom Pl KY16 29 G5
Angus St DD2 13 H1
Ann St DD3 15 E3
Annandale Av DD3 6 A4
Annfield Rd DD1 14 B5
Annfield Row DD1 14 B5
Annfield St DD1 14 B5
Anson Pl KY16 27 C5
Anson Walk KY16 27 D5
Anstruther Rd, Dundee DD4 15 G1
Anstruther Rd, St Andrews KY16 29 G5
Anton Dr DD5 17 H4
Apollo Way DD2 12 C4
Appleby Pl DD3 6 A4
Applecross Gdns DD2 12 C2
Arbroath Rd, Broughty Ferry DD5 17 F3
Arbroath Rd, Carnoustie DD7 21 G4
Arbroath Rd, Dundee DD4 15 F3
Arbuthnott Loan DD5 18 A2
Archer St DD5 17 H4
Ardestie Pl DD5 19 E2
Ardestie St DD5 18 D2
Ardminish Pl DD4 9 F6
Ardmore Av DD5 18 C3
Ardownie DD5 11 F5
Ardownie Pl DD5 19 E2
Ardownie Quarry DD5 11 F4
Ardownie St DD5 18 D2
Argyle Ct KY16 29 E3
Argyle St, Dundee DD4 15 F1
Argyle St, St Andrews KY16 29 E3
Arisaig Gdns DD2 12 C3
Arklay Pl DD3 15 F1
Arklay St DD3 15 E2
Arklay Ter DD3 15 E1
Armit Pl KY16 28 C6
Armour Pl DD4 7 H5
Arnhall Dr DD2 13 G5
Arnhall Gdns DD2 13 G5
Arran Dr DD2 13 F2
Arrol Rd DD2 12 C1
Arthur St DD3 3 C1
Arthurstone Ter DD4 15 F3
Artillery La DD1 3 B4
Ash La DD1 14 C4
Ash St DD1 14 C4
Ashbank Rd DD2 14 A4
Ashgrove DD5 19 G1
Ashkirk Gdns DD4 9 E6
Ashkirk Pl DD4 8 D6
Ashlar La KY15 25 C2
Ashlar Pk KY15 25 C2
Ashludie Fm DD5 11 G6
Ashludie Mews DD5 19 G1
Ashludie Ter DD5 19 H1
Ashmore St DD3 6 C4
Ashton Ter DD3 6 B1
Atholl Glen Yd DD4 7 F3
Atholl St DD2 13 H2
Auchencairn Pl DD5 18 D2
Auchinblae Pl DD3 5 G2
Auchrannie Ter DD4 16 B4
Auchterlonie Ct KY16 29 F5
Auld Burn Pk KY16 29 F4
Auld Burn Rd KY16 29 F4
Avon Cres DD5 18 C2
Avon Pl DD5 18 C1
Avondale Ter DD5 17 G4

Baberton Ct DD2 5 H4
Back Dykes DD6 24 D1
Back Lebanon KY15 25 C1
Backhill Rd DD2 13 G3
Backmuir Dr DD2 4 C2
Badenoch Pl DD4 8 D6
Baffin St DD4 15 G3
Baffin Ter DD4 15 G3
Baird Av DD2 5 H5
Baker La KY16 29 F3
Baker Pl KY16 26 D4
Baker Rd DD5 17 F1
Balbeggie Pl DD4 16 D3
Balbeggie St DD4 16 D3
Balbeggie Ter DD4 17 E3
Balcairn Pl DD4 16 D2
Balcarres Ter DD4 16 D3
Baldovan Rd DD3 6 B3
Baldovan Ter DD4 15 G2
Baldovie Gdns DD4 17 F3
Baldovie Ind Est DD4 17 E1
Baldovie Pl DD4 17 F3
Baldovie Rd DD4 17 F1
Baldovie Ter DD4 17 E3
Baldragon Vw DD3 6 A2
Balerno Pl DD4 16 D3
Balerno St DD4 16 C3
Balfield Rd DD3 14 A2
Balfour Pl, Dundee DD7 21 F4
Balfour Pl, St Andrews KY16 29 G3
Balfour St DD1 3 A4
Balgarthno Pl DD2 13 E1
Balgarthno Rd DD2 12 D1
Balgarthno St DD2 13 E1
Balgarthno Ter DD2 13 E1
Balgarvie Cres KY15 25 B1
Balgarvie Ct KY15 25 B2
Balgarvie Rd KY15 25 A1
Balgavies Av DD4 16 B4
Balgavies Pl DD4 16 B4
Balgay Ct DD2 13 E3
Balgay Rd DD2 14 A4
Balgay St DD2 13 H2
Balgayview Gdns DD3 14 A3
Balgillo Rd DD5 17 F3
Balgillo Rd East DD5 17 H2
Balgowan Av DD3 6 B3
Balgowan Dr DD3 6 C3
Balgowan Pl DD3 6 D3
Balgowan Sq DD3 6 C3
Balgowan Ter DD3 6 C3
Balgray Pl DD4 7 E6
Balgray St DD3 6 D6
Ballantrae Gdns DD4 16 D2
Ballantrae Pl DD4 16 C2
Ballantrae Rd DD4 16 C2
Ballantrae Ter DD4 16 C2
Ballater Pl DD4 17 E3
Ballinard Gdns DD5 17 G4
Ballinard Rd DD5 17 F4
Ballindean Cres DD4 16 C3
Ballindean Pl DD4 16 C3
Ballindean Rd DD4 16 B3
Ballindean Ter DD4 16 C2
Ballingall Ind Est DD1 14 C4
Balloch Pl DD4 17 E3
Ballochmyle Dr DD4 7 H5
Ballumbie Braes DD4 8 D6
Ballumbie Ct DD4 8 D6
Ballumbie Dr DD4 8 D6
Ballumbie Gdns DD4 8 D5
Ballumbie Mdws DD4 8 D6
Ballumbie Pl DD4 8 D6
Ballumbie Rd DD4 8 D3
Ballumbie Vw DD4 8 D5
Balmachie Rd DD7 21 E3
Balmedie Dr DD4 16 C3
Balmerino Pl DD4 16 D3
Balmerino Rd DD4 16 D2
Balmoral Av DD4 17 E2
Balmoral Gdns DD4 17 E2
Balmoral Pl DD4 16 D2
Balmoral Ter DD4 16 D2
Balmore St DD4 15 F2
Balmossie Av DD5 18 C3
Balmossie Pl DD5 18 C3
Balmuir Pl DD3 6 D3
Balmuir Rd DD3 6 D3
Balmullo Pl DD4 16 C3
Balmullo Sq DD4 16 C2
Balmyle Rd DD5 17 F4
Balnacarron Av KY16 28 C5
Balrymonth Ct KY16 29 E5
Balshando Pl DD2 6 A6
Baltic Gdns DD2 14 B6
Balunie Av DD4 16 C3
Balunie Cres DD4 16 C2
Balunie Dr DD4 16 C2
Balunie Gdns DD4 17 E3
Balunie Pl DD4 17 E3
Balunie St DD4 17 E3
Balunie Ter DD4 17 E3
Baluniefield Rd DD4 17 E3
Baluniefield Trading Est DD4 17 E2
Banchory Rd DD4 16 D3
Bank Av DD3 6 B5
Bank Mill Rd DD1 14 B4
Bank St, Cupar KY15 25 C1
Bank St, Dundee DD1 3 D3
Bank St, Monifieth DD5 19 E3
Bank St, Newport-on-Tay DD6 23 G1
Banknowe Av DD6 24 D2
Banknowe Dr DD6 24 D2
Banknowe Gro DD6 24 D2
Banknowe Rd DD6 24 D2
Banknowe Ter DD6 24 D2
Barassie Ct DD2 5 H4
Barlow Av DD5 17 F1
Barlow Pk DD5 17 F1
Barnes Av DD4 6 D6
Barns Neuk DD4 7 F3
Barns of Claverhouse Rd DD4 7 F4
Barra Ter DD4 7 G4
Barrack Rd DD3 3 B1
Barrack St DD1 3 C2
Barry By-Pass DD7 20 A5
Barry Rd DD7 20 A4
Bassaguard Ind Est KY16 29 E4
Bath St DD5 17 H6
Baxter Park Ct DD4 15 G2
Baxter Park Glebe DD4 15 G3
Baxter Park Ter DD4 15 G2
Baxter St DD2 14 B4
Bay Rd DD6 22 A6
Bayfield Gdns DD5 17 F5
Bayfield Rd DD5 17 G5
Bayne Sq DD3 14 D2
Bayview Pl DD5 19 G1
Bayview Rd DD2 12 C5
Beach Cres DD5 17 H6
Beach La DD5 17 F5
Beach Rd DD6 22 C4
Beaufort Cl KY16 26 E3
Beaufort Cres KY16 26 E3
Beauly Av DD3 6 D4
Beauly Cres DD3 6 D4
Beauly Sq DD3 6 D4
Beaumont Cres DD5 17 G4
Beaumont Ter DD5 17 G3
Beech Bank KY15 25 D2
Beechgrove DD5 19 G1
Beechwood Pk DD7 20 D3
Beechwood Ter DD2 13 H5
Beechwood Ter East DD6 23 F4
Beechwood Ter West DD6 23 E4
Belfield Gdns KY15 25 C2
Bell St, Dundee DD1 3 C2
Bell St, St Andrews KY16 29 F3
Bell St, Tayport DD6 24 C1
Bellefield Av DD1 14 C6
Bellfield St DD1 14 C5
Bellisle Dr DD4 16 B2
Bellisle Pl DD4 16 A3
Bellrock Sq DD5 17 G6
Bells La DD5 17 H6
Belltree Gdns DD5 18 C2
Belsize Pl DD5 16 D5
Belsize Rd DD5 16 D5
Ben Hogan Pl DD7 20 C5
Benholm Pl DD3 5 G2
Bennan Gdns DD5 17 H4
Benvie Rd DD2 14 B3
Berry Pl KY16 28 B5
Berwick Dr DD4 8 A5
Beryl St DD4 17 E2
Bingham Ter DD4 15 G2
Binsted Av DD3 6 C5
Birchwood Pl DD2 14 A4
Birkdale Pl DD3 5 G3
Birkhill Av DD6 22 B5
Birkhill Pl DD2 4 C3
Birks Ter DD4 7 H5
Birnam Pl DD2 13 G3
Birsay Gdns DD5 17 H3
Bishopgate KY15 25 C1
Black St DD2 14 B4
Blacklaw Dr DD2 4 C2
Blacklock Cres DD4 7 H5
Blackness Av DD2 14 A5
Blackness Ct DD1 14 B4
Blackness Rd DD1,DD2 13 G5
Blackness St DD1 14 B4
Blackness Trading Precinct*, Douglas St DD1 14 C4
Blackscroft DD4 3 F1
Blackwood Ct DD2 13 G3
Blaikies Mews DD3 15 E2
Blair Gdns DD5 18 A2
Blairfield Rd DD2 4 C2
Blairfield Ter DD2 4 C3
Blake Av DD5 17 G4
Blake Pl DD5 17 G4
Blake St DD5 17 G4
Blalowan Gdns KY15 25 C3
Blalowan Pk KY15 25 C3
Blantyre Pl DD3 6 B4
Blenheim Pl KY16 26 C4
Blinshall St DD1 3 A2
Blyth Ct DD6 23 F2
Blyth St, Dundee DD2 14 B4
Blyth St, Newport-on-Tay DD6 23 F2
Boase Av KY16 29 F4
Boat Brae DD6 23 F3
Boat Rd DD6 23 F3
Bobber Wynd KY15 25 D2
Bobby Jones Pl KY16 28 D6
Bogward Rd KY16 28 B5
Bonar Ct KY15 25 C2
Bonella St DD7 21 F4
Boniface Gdns DD2 12 C5
Boniface Pl DD2 12 C5
Boniface Rd DD2 12 C5
Bonnethill Ct DD3 3 C1
Bonnybank Rd DD1 15 E3
Bonnygate KY15 25 C2
Bonnyrigg Pl DD4 15 H1
Bonspiel Gdns DD5 18 B4
Bonvil Row KY15 25 B1
Borthwick Pl KY16 26 E2
Bowbridge Ct DD3 14 D2
Bowbridge Ind Est DD3 14 D2
Bowbridge Pl DD3 14 D2
Bower Mill La DD3 5 G3
Bowling Green Rd KY15 25 D1
Boyack Cres DD5 19 G1
Boyd Pl DD5 18 A5
Boysack Gdns DD5 17 G3
Brackenbrae DD5 17 G5
Brackens Rd DD3 5 H2
Bradbury St DD3 6 A3
Braefoot DD7 20 D3
Braehead KY15 25 D1
Braehead Dr DD7 21 E3
Braehead*, Metheven Walk DD2 14 A2
Braemar Gdns DD5 18 B2
Braeside Rd DD6 23 E4
Braid Cres KY16 29 H5
Braid Rd DD6 24 D1
Brantwood Av DD3 14 B2
Brantwood Pl DD3 14 B1
Brewery La DD1 14 C4
Brewster Pl KY16 29 H5
Briarwood Ter DD2 13 H5
Bridge La DD5 18 C4
Bridge St, Broughty Ferry DD5 18 C4
Bridge St, Newport-on-Tay DD6 23 F4
Bridge St, St Andrews KY16 29 E4
Bridgehead Pl DD6 22 B6
Bridgend St DD4 16 A2
Bright St DD2 13 H1
Brighton Rd KY15 25 A4
Brington Pl DD4 16 B4
Brington Rd DD4 16 B4
Britannia Dr DD4 8 D6
Broad St DD6 24 D1
Broadford Ter DD5 18 A4
Broadlands DD7 21 H3
Brochtie Ct DD5 17 H6
Brodick Walk DD4 8 A5
Brook Ct DD1 14 C4
Brook St, Broughty Ferry DD5 17 G5
Brook St, Dundee DD1 3 A3
Brook St, Monifieth DD5 19 G2
Broomfaulds Av KY16 28 D5
Broomhill Ct DD5 11 G6
Broomhill Dr DD5 11 G6

Broomhill Rd DD2 5 G6
Broomlee Rd DD2 13 F2
Brothock Gdns DD4 15 H1
Brougham Gdns DD4 15 F2
Broughty Ferry Ct DD4 17 F2
Broughty Ferry Rd DD4 15 F3
Broughty Ferry Walk DD4 17 F2
Brown Constable St DD4 15 F2
Brown St, Broughty Ferry DD5 17 G6
Brown St, Carnoustie DD7 20 D4
Brown St, Dundee DD1 3 A2
Brownhill Pl DD2 13 E1
Brownhill Rd DD2 13 E1
Brownhill St DD2 13 F1
Browns Wynd DD6 24 E2
Bruce Ct DD7 21 F5
Bruce Dr DD7 20 D3
Bruce Embankment KY16 29 E2
Bruce Rd DD3 6 C5
Bruce St, Dundee DD3 14 D2
Bruce St, St Andrews KY16 29 F5
Brunel Rd DD2 12 C1
Buchanan Gdns KY16 28 C4
Buchanan St DD4 15 F2
Bucklemaker Ct DD3 14 D2
Bucklers Wynd DD5 9 H1
Bucklerscroft DD5 9 G1
Buddon Dr, Carnoustie DD7 20 C5
Buddon Dr, Monifieth DD5 19 G1
Buddon Pl DD7 20 C5
Bughties Rd DD5 18 A5
Buick Pl DD4 16 A2
Burgess St DD3 14 D2
Burn St DD3 6 B3
Burnaby St DD2 13 F5
Burnhaven Gdns DD5 16 D3
Burnside KY16 26 E2
Burnside Ct, Cupar KY15 25 C1
Burnside Ct, Dundee DD2 14 A2
Burnside East KY15 25 C2
Burnside Gdns, Carnoustie DD7 21 E4
Burnside Gdns, Lochee DD2 14 A2
Burnside North KY15 25 C1
Burnside Rd, Barry DD7 20 A5
Burnside Rd, Invergowrie DD2 12 C5
Burnside St, Carnoustie DD7 21 E4
Burnside St, Lochee DD2 13 H2
Burnside Walk DD2 14 A2
Burnview DD3 6 C3
Burrelton Gdns DD3 5 H2
Buttars Loan DD2 13 F2
Buttars Pl DD2 13 F1
Buttars Rd DD2 13 E1
Buttars St DD2 13 F1
Buttars Ter DD2 13 F1
Butter Wynd DD6 24 E2
Butterburn Ct DD3 14 D2
Butterburn Sq DD3 14 D2
Butts Wynd KY16 29 F3
Byron Cres DD3 14 B2
Byron St DD3 14 B2
Byron Ter DD3 14 C2

Caenlochan Pl DD5 17 E4
Caenlochan Rd DD5 17 F4
Caesar Av DD7 21 G3
Caird Av DD3 14 D1
Caird Ter DD3 14 D1
Cairnhill Gdns KY16 28 B6
Cairnsden Gdns KY16 28 C6
Calcutta La DD1 3 F3
Calder Cres DD5 17 H3
Calderwood Cl DD2 14 A1
Caldrum St DD3 14 D2
Caldrum Ter DD3 14 D2
Caledon St DD1 15 H3
Callender Gdns DD4 15 F3
Camberwell Ct DD4 8 C6
Cambridge St DD2 13 G4
Cambustay Gdns DD5 18 C4
Camerons Cl DD1 3 D2
Campbell Cres KY15 25 E3
Campbell St DD3 14 B2
Camperdown Ind Pk DD2 5 F5
Camperdown Rd DD3 6 A4
Camperdown St, Broughty Ferry DD5 17 G5
Camperdown St, Dundee DD1 3 F2
Camperdown St, Lochee DD2 13 H2
Campfield Gdns DD5 18 A4
Campfield Rd DD5 18 A4
Campfield Sq DD5 18 B4
Camphill Pl DD5 17 H5
Camphill Rd DD5 17 H5
Camus Ct DD7 21 E4
Camus St DD7 21 E4
Candle La DD1 3 E2
Canisp Cres DD2 12 C3
Canning Pl DD3 14 D1
Canning St DD3 14 D1
Canongate KY16 28 D5
Cant Cres KY16 28 B5
Carberry Cres DD4 8 B5
Cardean St DD4 15 F2
Cardoness Walk DD4 8 B6
Cardross Pl DD4 7 E6
Cardross St DD3 15 E1
Carlochie Pl DD4 16 B4
Carlogie Rd DD7 21 F1
Carlunie Rd DD2 5 H6
Carlunie St DD2 5 H6
Carmichael Ct DD3 14 D3
Carmichael Gdns DD3 14 D3
Carmichael St DD3 14 D2
Carmyllie Pl DD5 19 F1
Carnbane Dr DD5 18 A2
Carnegie Sq DD3 15 E3
Carnegie St DD3 15 E2
Carnegie Twrs DD3 15 E3
Carnoustie Ct DD2 5 H4
Carolina Ct DD1 15 H3
Carolina St DD1 15 H3
Carradale Dr DD4 9 E6
Carron Pl, Dundee DD5 18 A3
Carron Pl, St Andrews KY16 28 B5
Carse Pl DD2 12 B6
Carselea Rd DD2 12 B4
Carseview Gdns DD2 13 G5
Carslogie Rd KY15 25 A2
Cart Pl DD2 13 E3
Cassidy Walk DD4 8 A5
Castle App DD5 17 H6
Castle Bank DD6 23 E4
Castle Brae DD6 23 E4
Castle La DD5 18 A6
Castle Rd DD6 24 D1
Castle St, Broughty Ferry DD5 18 A6
Castle St, Cupar KY15 25 D1
Castle St, Dundee DD1 3 D3
Castle St, Tayport DD6 24 D1
Castle Ter, Broughty Ferry DD5 18 A6
Castle Ter, Dundee DD4 7 G6
Castle Ter, Tayport DD6 24 D1
Castlebank Gdns KY15 25 D1
Castlebank Rd KY15 25 D1
Castlecary Gdns DD4 8 B6
Castlefield KY15 25 D1
Castlehill KY15 25 D2
Castlehill Pl KY15 25 D2
Castleroy Cres DD5 18 A4
Castleroy Rd DD5 18 A4
Castleton Pl DD5 17 G3
Castlewood Av DD3 7 E3
Castlewood Brae DD3 7 E3
Caswell Cl DD3 15 E3
Catherine St DD4 15 F2
Catterline Cres DD3 5 G2
Cawdor Ct DD2 5 H4
Cedar Gro DD5 17 H4
Cedar Rd DD5 17 H4
Cedarwood Dr DD2 14 A1
Ceres Cres DD5 18 A3
Ceres Rd KY15 25 D3
Chalk Hill Ct DD4 8 C6
Challum Cres DD5 18 D2
Challum Pl DD5 18 D2
Chalmers St DD4 15 G1
Chamberlain St KY16 29 E4
Chambers Pl KY16 28 B5
Chapel Rd DD5 9 H1
Chapel St DD1 3 D2
Chapman Dr DD7 21 G2
Charles Bowman Av DD4 7 G3
Charles St DD7 21 E5
Charleston Dr DD2 12 D3
Charleston Rd DD2 13 E1
Charleston St DD2 13 E1
Charlotte Cl DD3 6 B5
Charlotte Pl DD3 6 B4
Charlotte St DD3 6 B4
Cherry La KY15 25 D2
Chestnut Grn DD4 9 F5
Chevaliers Pend DD4 7 F4
Cheviot Cres DD4 7 H3
Cheviot Rise DD4 7 H3
Chirnside Pl DD4 9 E6
Christian Rd DD5 16 C5
Church Ct DD5 17 G5
Church Sq KY16 29 F3
Church St, Broughty Ferry DD5 17 G6
Church St, Carnoustie DD7 21 G4
Church St, Dundee DD3 15 E2
Church St, Monifieth DD5 19 F2
Church St, St Andrews KY16 29 F3
Churchhill Vw*, Meadowside Rd KY15 25 D3
Churchill Cres KY16 29 F5
Churchill Pl DD5 18 A5
City Quay Shopping Centre DD1 3 F2
City Rd, Dundee DD2 14 A3
City Rd, St Andrews KY16 29 E3
City Sq DD1 3 D3
Clarence Rd DD4 15 H2
Clarendon Dr DD2 14 A6
Clatto Gdns DD3 5 G2
Clatto Pl KY16 29 E4
Clattowoods Dr DD3 5 F2
Clattowoods Pl DD3 5 F2
Clattowoods Rd DD3 5 G2
Clattowoods Ter DD3 5 G2
Claverhouse East Ind Pk DD4 7 H3
Claverhouse Old Rd DD4 7 E3
Claverhouse Rd DD4 7 E3
Claverhouse West Ind Pk DD4 7 G3
Clay Rd KY16 26 F2
Claybraes KY16 29 E5
Clayhills Dr DD2 13 E4
Clayhills Gdns DD2 4 B2
Clayhills Gro DD2 13 E5
Claypotts Castle Gdns DD5 17 F3
Claypotts Ct DD5 17 F3
Claypotts Pl DD5 17 F3
Claypotts Rd DD5 17 F3
Claypotts Ter DD5 17 F4
Cleghorn St DD2 14 B4
Clement Park Pl DD2 13 H1
Clement Park Rd DD2 13 H1
Clement Park Ter DD2 13 H1
Clepington Ct DD3 15 E1
Clepington Rd DD3 6 A6
Clepington St DD3 15 E2
Cleveland Circle DD4 16 A2
Clifden Blue Ct DD4 8 C6
Cliffburn Gdns DD5 17 G3
Clinkerheel Dr DD2 4 B2
Clinton Ter DD5 17 F4
Clive Rd DD3 6 C5
Clive St DD4 15 F1
Cloan Rd DD3 6 B4
Clovis Duveau Dr DD2 12 D4
Clunie Gdns DD3 5 H2
Clyde Pl DD2 13 F3
Coal Rd KY15 25 D2
Cobden Ct DD3 14 A3
Cobden Pl DD2 14 A3
Cobden St DD3 14 A2
Coldside Rd DD3 14 C1
Coldstream Dr DD4 9 E6
Colin Gibson Dr DD5 18 D1
Colinton Pl DD2 14 A4
Collace Cres DD3 6 A2
College St KY16 29 F3
Collier St DD7 21 E4
Collingwood Cres DD5 18 C4
Collingwood Pl DD5 18 D4
Collingwood St DD5 18 C4
Colliston Dr DD5 18 A2
Colonsay Ter DD4 7 G4
Commerce St KY15 25 A4
Commercial Ct DD1 3 E3
Commercial St DD1 3 D2
Commonty Rd DD6 24 C1
Condie Ct KY16 29 F3
Condor Ct DD7 21 F3
Coniston Ter DD3 6 C4
Connel Ter DD3 6 D3
Constable Acre KY15 25 B1
Constable Cres KY15 25 B1
Constable La DD5 17 F5
Constable St DD4 3 F1
Constitution Cres DD3 3 B1
Constitution Ct DD3 14 D3
Constitution Rd DD3 3 B1
Constitution St DD3 14 D3
Constitution Ter DD3 14 D3
Corbie Dr DD7 20 B4
Corran Gdns DD5 17 H4
Corso St DD2 14 B5
Cortachy Circle DD5 19 E1
Cortachy Cres DD5 17 H2
Cottage Pl DD5 17 H6
Cotton Rd DD3 15 E2
Coupar Angus Rd DD2 4 A2
Coupar St DD2 14 A2
Court House Sq DD1 3 B2
Court St DD3 15 F2
Court St North DD3 15 F1
Coutties Wynd DD1 3 D3
Covenanters Pend DD4 7 F4
Cow Brae KY15 25 D3
Cowan Pl*, Cowan St DD4 15 F2
Cowan St DD4 15 F2
Cowgate, Dundee DD1 3 D2
Cowgate, Tayport DD6 24 E2
Cox Gdns DD3 6 A3
Cox St DD3 6 B3
Craig La DD6 24 D2
Craig Pl DD7 21 G3
Craig Rd DD6 24 D2
Craigard Gdns DD2 13 E2
Craigard Rd DD2 13 F1
Craighead Cres DD6 23 G1
Craighead Rd DD6 23 G2
Craighill Ct DD4 7 H6
Craigie Av DD4 16 A4
Craigie Dr DD4 16 C5
Craigie Pl DD4 16 C5
Craigie St DD4 15 F2
Craigiebarn Rd DD4 16 C4
Craigielea Pl DD4 16 A2
Craigielea Ter DD4 16 A2
Craigievar Walk DD4 8 B5
Craigmill Gdns DD7 21 F2
Craigmill Rd DD3 6 A1
Craigmore St DD3 6 C4
Craigmount Av DD2 13 F2
Craigmount Pl DD2 13 F1
Craigmount Rd DD2 13 F2
Craigmount Ter DD2 13 F1
Craigowan Rd DD2 13 E1
Craigowl Rd DD2 5 H6
Craigowl St DD2 5 H6
Craigrossie Pl*, Dundee St DD7 21 E4
Craigshannoch Rd DD6 22 A6
Craigton Gdns DD5 19 E1
Craigview Ct DD6 24 D2
Crail Pl DD5 18 B3
Crails La KY16 29 F3
Cramond Pl DD4 8 B6
Crathes Way DD5 18 A2
Crathie Pl DD4 16 C3
Crawford Gdns KY16 28 D5
Crawford Pl DD5 16 D4
Crescent La DD4 15 F3
Crescent St DD4 15 F3
Crichton St DD1 3 D3
Crichton Way KY15 25 E3
Cromarty Dr DD2 13 G2
Crombie Ter DD4 16 A4
Cross La DD1 3 B4
Cross Row DD1 3 A4
Cross St, Broughty Ferry DD5 18 A6
Cross St, Tayport DD6 24 E3
Crossgate KY15 25 D2
Crosshill Ter DD6 22 C5
Cullen Pl DD4 16 C3
Cults Gdns DD5 16 D3
Cumnock Pl DD4 7 H5
Cunningham St DD4 15 F3
Cupar Mills KY15 25 C3
Cupar Rd, Cupar Muir KY15 25 A4
Cupar Rd, Newport-on-Tay DD6 23 F2
Cupar Rd, St Andrews KY16 27 A8
Cupar Rd, Tayport DD6 24 D4
Cupar Trading Est KY15 25 F1
Curling Pond Ct KY15 25 E1
Cuthberts Brae DD6 23 E3
Cuthberts Rd DD6 23 E4
Cuthlie Pl KY16 28 B5
Cuthrie St DD7 21 G4
Cynicus Pl KY16 26 E2

Dalcraig Cres DD4 16 C4
Dalgairn Cres KY15 25 C1
Dalgetty Ct DD2 4 B2
Dalgleish Apts DD3 3 A1
Dalgleish Gdns KY15 25 C1
Dalgleish Rd DD4 16 A4
Dalgleish St DD6 24 D1
Dalhousie Gdns DD5 19 G2
Dalhousie Pk DD5 19 G1
Dalhousie Rd DD5 18 B5
Dalhousie St, Carnoustie DD7 21 F3
Dalhousie St, Monifieth DD5 19 G2
Dalkeith Rd DD4 15 G1
Dallfield Ct DD3 3 C1
Dalmahoy Dr DD2 5 G4
Dalrymple Pl DD2 13 F3
Dalrymple St DD2 13 G2
Dalrymple Ter DD2 13 G3
Daniel St DD1 3 A3
Dargarvel Gdns DD4 8 B6
Dargie Rd DD2 12 C5
Darvel Pl DD4 7 H5
Davan Pl DD5 17 H3
David Robertson St DD4 15 F1
David St DD5 17 H6
David Wilson Pk KY16 26 E1
Davidson St DD5 17 G4
Dawson Cres DD5 18 C3
Dawson Pl DD5 16 D4
Dawson Rd DD5 16 D4
Dayton Dr DD2 5 G5
Dean Av DD4 16 A4
Deanbank St DD2 13 G3
Deans Ct KY16 29 G3
Dee Gdns DD2 12 D2
Dee Pl DD2 12 D2
Deepdale Pl DD5 17 G4
Deerpark Rd DD4 15 H2
Delta Centre DD2 12 D4
Dempster Ct KY16 29 F4
Dempster Ter KY16 29 F4
Denhead Cres DD2 12 D1
Denoon Ter DD2 13 F2
Dens Brae DD1 3 F1
Dens Rd DD3 14 D1
Dens St DD4 3 F1
Derby St DD3 14 D2
Derwent Av DD3 6 C4
Deveron Cres DD2 12 D2
Deveron Ter DD2 12 D2
Devonlea Rd DD6 22 A6
Dick St, Broughty Ferry DD5 18 A5
Dick St, Monifieth DD5 19 G1
Dickson Av DD2 13 E3
Dighty Gdns DD2 12 D2
Dighty Pl DD2 13 E2
Dobson Dr DD7 21 F2
Dochart Ter DD2 13 F3
Dock St DD1 3 E3
Donald St DD2 13 G2
Donalds La DD2 13 F1
Donaldson Gdns KY16 28 D3
Dons Rd DD3 14 D3
Doocot Rd KY16 28 C5
Doon Ter DD4 16 A2
Dores Dr DD5 18 A3
Dornie Pl DD2 12 C3
Dornoch Pl DD5 18 A4
Double Dykes Rd KY16 29 E3
Dougall St DD6 24 D1
Douglas Ct*, Douglas St DD1 14 C4
Douglas Gdns DD7 20 D3
Douglas Rd DD4 16 B4
Douglas St DD1 3 A2
Douglas Ter, Broughty Ferry DD5 17 F5
Douglas Ter, Dundee DD3 14 C3
Douglasfield Cres DD4 16 C2
Dow St DD1 14 C5
Downfield Ct DD2 5 H4
Downie Mill DD5 11 G2
Downie Park Pl DD3 6 D5
Downie Park Rd DD3 6 D6
Downie Pk DD3 7 E6
Downieken DD5 11 H1
Doyle Pl DD2 13 H2
Dronley Av DD2 4 B2
Dronley Rd DD2 4 C2
Dronley Ter DD2 4 B2
Drum Rd KY15 25 A4
Drum Well KY15 25 A4
Drumcarrow Rd KY16 29 E4
Drumdryan Pl KY15 25 C4
Drumgeith Rd DD4 16 C2
Drumlanrig Dr DD4 16 A2
Drumlanrig Pl DD4 16 A3
Drumlithie Pl DD3 5 H2
Drumlochie Gdns DD5 18 B2
Drummond Ct KY15 25 B3
Drummond St DD3 14 C3
Drumsturdy Rd DD5 9 F6
Dryburgh Cres DD2 5 G6

Dryburgh Gdns DD2 5 G6
Dryburgh Ind Est DD2 5 H5
Dryburgh Pl DD2 5 F6
Dryburgh St DD2 5 G6
Dryburgh Ter DD2 12 B5
Drysdale Gdns KY15 25 B2
Dudhope Crescent Rd DD1 3 B1
Dudhope Ct DD1 14 B4
Dudhope Garden Steps DD3 14 B3
Dudhope Pl DD3 3 C1
Dudhope St DD1 3 C1
Dudhope Ter DD3 14 B3
Duff St DD4 15 G1
Duffus Ct DD4 7 F3
Dunalistair Gdns DD5 17 H5
Dunavon Gdns DD3 6 A2
Dunbar Pk DD4 8 C6
Duncan Pl DD3 6 B3
Duncan St DD3 6 B3
Duncan Ter DD3 6 B3
Duncarse Pl DD2 12 D2
Duncarse Rd DD2 12 D2
Duncraig Rd DD2 12 D2
Dundarroch Gdns DD5 18 B5
Dundas St DD5 17 G6
Dundee Airport DD2 13 F6
Dundee Rd DD5 16 D5
Dundee Rd West DD5 16 C5
Dundee St DD7 21 E4
Dundee Technology Pk DD2 12 C3
Dundonald Ct DD3 15 E1
Dundonald St DD3 15 E2
Dunearn St DD5 18 A3
Dunedin Pk KY16 26 E2
Dunholm Pl DD2 12 D2
Dunholm Rd DD2 12 D2
Dunholm St DD2 12 D1
Dunholm Ter DD2 13 E2
Dunkeld Pl DD2 13 G3
Dunmore Dr DD2 13 G5
Dunmore Gdns DD2 13 F5
Dunmore St DD3 6 C4
Dunolly Pl KY16 29 G4
Dunottar Pl DD5 17 E4
Dunrobin Walk DD4 8 B5
Duns Cres DD4 8 D6
Dunshelt Rd DD5 18 A3
Dunsinane Av DD2 5 H6
Dunsinane Ind Est, Dundee DD2 5 H6
Duntrune Rd DD4 7 H1
Duntrune Ter DD5 17 F4
Dunvegan Rd DD5 18 A3
Dura St DD4 15 F2
Durham St DD5 19 E3
Durness Ter DD2 12 C3
Durris Loan DD5 18 A2
Dykehead Pl DD4 15 E2
Dysart Pl DD5 18 B3

Eadies Rd DD1 15 E3
Earl Grey Pl DD1 3 E4
Earl St DD2 13 H1
Earlshall Rd KY16 26 D3
Earlston Av DD4 8 D6
Earlston Pl DD7 21 G4
Earn Cres DD2 12 D3
Earn Pl DD2 12 D3
Eassie Ter DD2 13 G3
Eassons Angle DD1 14 B4
East Bri KY15 25 D2
East Camperdown St DD1 15 G4
East Dennison Rd DD4 15 H1
East Dock Retail Pk DD4 3 F1
East Dock St DD1 3 F2
East Grange St DD5 19 E2
East Haddon Rd DD4 16 A4
East Hendersons Wynd DD1 3 B3
East Home St DD5 17 G5
East Links Pl DD5 18 A5
East Marketgait DD1 3 E1
East Navarre St DD5 18 D3
East Queen St DD6 23 G1
East Rd, Cupar KY15 25 D2
East Rd, Dundee DD2 4 B5
East Row DD7 21 H4
East School Rd DD3 6 B5
East Scores KY16 29 G3
East Scotscraig La DD2 5 H4
East Station Pl DD6 23 G2
East Whale La DD1 3 F1
Eastgait Rise DD6 24 E2
Eastwell Gdns DD2 14 A2
Eastwell Rd DD3 14 A2
Eddie Ct KY16 29 E4
Eden Pk KY15 25 E1
Eden St DD4 15 G3
Eden Ter DD4 15 G3
Eden Valley Bsns Pk KY15 25 F1
Edenbank Rd KY15 25 E2
Edison Pl DD2 5 G5
Edward Pl DD2 4 B2
Edward St DD1 14 C4
Edzell Ct DD2 5 H4
Edzell St DD5 18 A3
Elcho Dr DD5 18 B2
Elders Ct DD2 13 H2
Elgin Gdns DD3 6 C6
Elgin St DD3 6 C6
Elgin Ter DD3 6 C5
Elie Av DD5 18 B2
Elie Pl DD5 18 B2
Eliza St DD4 15 F2
Elizabeth Cres, Carnoustie DD7 21 F3
Elizabeth Cres, Newport-on-Tay DD6 23 G1
Elizabeth St DD6 24 D2
Ellen St DD1 15 E3
Ellengowan Dr DD4 15 G2
Ellice Pl KY16 29 E3
Ellieslea Rd DD5 17 F4
Elliot Ct DD2 13 G4
Elliot Rd DD2 13 G4
Elm Gro KY15 25 E2
Elm St DD2 14 A4
Elmgrove DD5 11 G6
Elmwood Dr DD2 13 G3
Elmwood Rd DD2 13 G2
Elsinore Pl DD5 19 G1
Elvan Pl DD2 13 H1
Emmock La DD3 7 F2
Emmock Pl DD3 6 C4
Emmock Rd, Downfield DD3 6 C1
Emmock Rd, Duntrune DD4 7 H1
Emmock Vw DD3 7 F3
Emmock Walk DD4 7 F2
Emmock Woods Dr DD4 7 F2
Ericht Pl DD2 13 F4
Ericht Rd DD6 22 C5
Eriskay Dr DD4 7 G4
Errol Rd DD2 12 A6
Erskine La DD5 17 H5
Erskine Rd DD6 24 E1
Erskine St DD4 15 F2
Erskine Ter DD5 19 F1
Eskdale Av DD3 6 A3
Ethie Ter DD5 17 G3
Ethiebeaton Pk DD5 11 E6
Ethiebeaton Ter DD5 19 E2
Etive Gdns DD2 12 D2
Eton St DD2 13 G4
Ettrick Cres DD2 5 G6
Euclid Cres DD1 3 C2
Euclid St DD1 3 C2
Exchange Ct DD1 3 E3
Exchange St DD1 3 E3
Explorer Rd DD2 12 C2

Fairbairn St DD3 15 E2
Fairfield Rd, Broughty Ferry DD5 17 E4
Fairfield Rd, Dundee DD3 6 C6
Fairfield St DD3 6 D6
Fairhurst Walk DD4 16 A2
Fairlie Ter DD3 5 H1
Fairmuir Rd DD3 6 D6
Fairmuir Sq DD3 6 D6
Fairmuir St DD3 6 D6
Fairmuir St North DD3 6 D6
Fairy La DD6 24 D1
Falkland Cres DD5 18 B2
Falkland Pl, Broughty Ferry DD5 18 B2
Falkland Pl, Kingoodie DD2 12 A6
Faraday Ct DD2 5 H5
Faraday St DD2 5 G5
Farington Gdns DD2 13 G5
Farington St DD2 13 G5
Farington Ter DD2 13 G5
Fenton Pl DD5 19 E1
Fenwick Pl DD4 16 C1
Ferguson Sq KY15 25 D2
Ferguson St DD4 15 F3
Fergusson Pl KY16 28 B4
Fern Pl KY16 26 C3
Ferndale Dr DD5 17 G4
Fernie Gdns DD5 18 B4
Ferrier St DD7 21 F4
Ferry Rd DD5 18 D3
Ferryfield KY15 25 B3
Fettercairn Dr DD5 18 B3
Fife Pk KY16 28 B4
Finavon Pl DD4 7 G4
Finavon St DD4 7 G4
Finavon Ter DD4 7 H4
Findale St DD4 16 A1
Findcastle Pl DD4 7 H4
Findcastle St DD4 7 H4
Findcastle Ter DD4 7 H4
Findchapel Pl DD4 8 A6
Findhorn Pl DD4 7 G3
Findhorn St DD4 7 G3
Findowrie Pl DD4 8 A5
Findowrie St DD4 7 H3
Finedon Ter DD4 7 H4
Finella Gdns DD4 7 H3
Finella Pl DD4 7 H3
Finella Ter DD4 8 A6
Fingask St DD3 14 C2
Finglas St DD4 8 A5
Finlaggan Cres DD4 16 A1
Finlaggan Pl DD4 16 A1
Finlaggan Ter DD4 16 A1
Finlarig Pl DD4 8 A6
Finlarig Ter DD4 8 A6
Finlow Pl DD4 8 A6
Finlow Ter DD4 8 A6
Finmore Pl DD4 8 A6
Finmore St DD4 8 A6
Fintry Cres DD4 7 H4
Fintry Dr DD4 7 G3
Fintry Gdns DD4 7 H4
Fintry Mains DD4 7 H4
Fintry Pl DD5 17 G4
Fintry Rd DD4 7 G4
Fintry Ter DD4 16 B1
Fintryside DD4 7 H4
Firth La DD1 3 F3
Fish Dock Rd DD1 16 A5
Fisher St DD5 17 G6
Flass Rd DD6 22 C5
Fleming Gdns East DD3 15 E1
Fleming Gdns North DD3 15 E1
Fleming Gdns South DD3 15 E1
Fleming Gdns West DD3 14 D1
Fleming Pl KY16 29 F4
Fleuchar St DD2 14 B4
Flights La DD2 13 H2
Foggyley Gdns DD2 14 A1
Foggyley Pl DD2 14 A1
Fontstane Cres DD5 19 E2
Fontstane Pl DD5 19 E2
Fontstane Rd DD5 19 E2
Fontstane St DD5 19 E2
Fontstane Ter DD5 19 E2
Forbes Pl KY16 28 B4
Fords La DD2 14 B5
Fordyce Ct KY16 29 E6
Forebank Rd DD1 15 E3
Forebank St DD1 3 E1
Forest Park Pl DD1 14 B4
Forest Park Rd DD1 14 B4
Forester St DD1 3 C2
Forfar Rd DD4 7 G6
Forgan Pl KY16 29 F5
Forgan St DD6 23 F4
Forgan Way DD6 23 E4
Forres Av DD3 6 D4
Forres Cres DD3 6 D4
Forrest St KY16 29 E5
Fort & Broch DD5 11 F3
Fort St, Broughty Ferry DD5 17 H6
Fort St, Dundee DD2 14 A5
Fortar Way DD5 18 A3
Forth Cres DD2 13 E2
Forth Pl DD2 13 E2
Forthill Dr DD5 17 H4
Forthill Pl DD5 17 H4
Forthill Rd DD5 17 H3
Forties Rd DD4 17 E1
Forum Shopping Centre DD1 3 D2
Foster Rd DD3 6 D5
Fothringham Dr DD5 19 E1
Foula Ter DD4 7 G4
Foundary La*, Tay St DD6 24 E2
Foundry La DD4 3 F1
Foundry Pl DD5 19 F2
Foundry Rd DD5 19 F3
Fountainbleau Dr DD4 7 G5
Fountainbrae DD5 19 G1
Fowler Rd DD5 17 F1
Fox St DD7 21 F4
Francis St DD3 14 C1
Fraser Av KY16 29 E5
Fraser St DD3 14 D2
Freddie Tait St KY16 29 F5
Frederick St DD3 6 B3
Freeman Gro KY16 26 D4
Front Lebanon KY15 25 C1
Fullarton St DD3 14 A2
Fulton Rd DD2 12 C1
Fyffe St DD1 14 B4
Fyne Rd DD5 18 A4
Fyvie Loan DD5 17 E3

Gairloch Rd DD5 18 A3
Gala Av DD2 13 F3
Gannochie Ter DD4 16 B4
Gannochy Ho KY16 29 F3
Garden Mill Pl DD3 5 G3
Gardeners La DD3 14 C3
Gardner St DD3 14 A2
Gardyne Pl DD4 16 C4
Gardyne Rd DD5 16 D4
Garland Pl, Dundee DD3 3 B1
Garland Pl, Newport-on-Tay DD6 23 F3
Garliebank Cres KY15 25 D4
Garnet Ter DD4 16 B4
Garry Pl DD3 6 A5
Garry Ter DD3 6 B4
Garten St DD5 18 A3
Garvock Pl DD3 5 H2
Gauldie Cres DD3 5 H1
Gauldie Ct DD3 5 H2
Gauldie Pl DD3 5 H2
Gauldie Ter DD3 6 A2
Gauldry Ter DD5 18 A3
Gellatly St DD1 3 E2
Gemini Cres DD2 12 C4
George Buckman Dr DD2 5 G5
George Pirie Way DD2 13 E4
George Pl DD2 12 C5
George St DD2 13 G1
Gib Gdns KY15 25 E1
Gibbs La DD2 13 H2
Gibson Pl KY16 29 E2
Gibson St DD7 20 C5
Gibson Ter DD4 15 F1
Gilchrist Row KY16 28 D5
Gillburn Rd DD3 6 B4
Gillespie Ter, Dundee DD4 7 F3
Gillespie Ter, St Andrews KY16 29 E2
Gillespie Wynd KY16 29 E2
Gillies Pl DD5 17 F3
Gillies Ter DD5 17 F4
Gilmour Pl DD2 13 H2
Gilroy Cotts DD3 3 B1
Gilston Pl DD5 18 A4
Girvan Gdns DD4 16 D1
Gladstone Sq DD6 24 E2
Glamis Ct DD2 13 E3
Glamis Dr DD2 13 F4
Glamis Pl DD2 13 F5
Glamis Rd DD2 13 G3
Glamis St DD3 15 E2
Glamis Ter DD2 13 F5
Glasclune Way DD5 18 A2
Glebe Gdns DD6 24 D3
Glebe Pl DD6 24 D3
Glebe Rd KY16 29 F4
Glenaffric Ter DD3 14 B1
Glenagnes Gdns DD2 14 A4
Glenagnes Rd DD2 14 B4
Glenagnes St DD2 14 A4
Glenclova Ter DD3 14 B1
Glenconner Dr DD4 7 H5
Glendevon Way DD5 18 A2
Gleneagles Av DD2 5 G4
Gleneagles La DD2 5 H4
Gleneagles Rd DD2 5 H4
Gleneagles St DD2 5 H4
Glenesk Av DD3 14 B1
Glenisla Ter DD3 14 B1
Glenleven Dr DD6 22 A6
Glenmarkie Ter DD3 14 B1
Glenmoy Av DD3 6 B6
Glenogil Av DD3 14 B1
Glenprosen Dr DD3 14 B1
Glenprosen Ter DD3 14 C1
Glentruim Ter DD3 6 B6
Godfrey St DD5 18 C3
Golf Av DD5 19 G2
Golf Cres DD6 24 E3
Golf Pl KY16 29 E2
Golf Rd DD6 24 E3
Golf St DD7 21 E5
Golspie Ter DD5 18 B4
Gordon Ct DD4 7 E3
Gordon Sq DD3 14 A2
Gordon St, Broughty Ferry DD5 18 C4
Gordon St, Dundee DD3 14 A2
Gorrie Ter DD3 6 A2
Gotterstone Av DD5 16 D3
Gotterstone Dr DD5 16 D3
Gourdie Cres DD2 13 E1
Gourdie Pl DD2 13 E1
Gourdie Rd DD2 12 D1
Gourdie St DD2 13 E1
Gourdie Ter DD2 13 E1
Gourlay Wynd KY16 29 E5
Gowrie Cres DD2 12 B5
Gowrie Ct DD2 13 E3
Gowrie St, Dundee DD2 14 B5
Gowrie St, Newport-on-Tay DD6 23 G2
Graham Ct DD4 7 E3
Graham Pl DD4 15 F3
Graham St DD4 7 E6
Graham Ter DD4 7 E6
Graham Wynd DD4 7 E6
Grampian Cl DD4 8 A5
Grampian Gdns DD4 8 A5
Granary Bsns Centre KY15 25 D2
Granary La DD6 23 F2
Grange Av DD5 19 E2
Grange Gait DD5 19 E1
Grange Gdns DD5 19 E1
Grange La DD5 19 E1
Grange Pl DD5 19 E3
Grange Rd, Dundee DD5 18 D2
Grange Rd, St Andrews KY16 29 G5
Grangehill Dr DD5 19 E2
Grannie Clarks Wynd KY16 29 E2
Granton Pl DD4 7 E6
Granton Ter DD4 7 E6
Gray St, Broughty Ferry DD5 17 H6
Gray St, Dundee DD2 13 G2
Grays La DD2 14 A2
Green La DD7 21 F4
Greenacre KY16 26 E1
Greenbank Pl DD2 14 A3
Greenbourne Gdns DD5 19 G2
Greendykes Rd DD4 16 A5
Greenfield Ct DD4 8 B6
Greenfield Pl DD1 14 C5
Greenlaw DD7 20 B4
Greenlaw Pl DD7 20 C4
Greenlee Dr DD2 13 F1
Greenmarket DD1 3 C4
Greenside Ct KY16 29 F4
Greenside Pl, Dundee DD6 24 E2
Greenside Pl, St Andrews KY16 29 F4
Greenstone Pl DD2 12 C2
Greenstone Ter DD2 12 C2
Gregory Ct DD6 24 D2
Gregory La KY16 29 G3
Gregory Pl KY16 29 G3
Grenada Brae DD6 23 G1
Grey St DD6 24 D1
Greyfriars Gdn KY16 29 F3
Greystane Rd DD2 12 B4
Greystane Ter DD2 12 B4
Grimmond La DD3 5 G3
Grosvenor Rd DD2 14 A5
Grove Rd DD5 17 F4
Gruinard Ter DD4 7 F4
Guardbridge Rd KY16 28 C2
Gullane Av DD2 5 H4
Gullane Pl DD2 5 H4
Gullane Rd DD2 5 H4
Gullane Ter DD2 5 H4
Guthrie Ct DD3 14 B1
Guthrie Pl KY16 29 F3
Guthrie St DD1 3 A3
Guthrie Ter DD5 18 C4

Hackston Pl KY15 25 C2
Haddington Av DD4 8 C6
Haddington Cres DD4 8 C6
Haddington Gdns DD4 8 C6
Haddington Pl DD4 8 C6
Haldane Av DD3 6 C4
Haldane Cres DD3 6 B4
Haldane La DD5 17 H5
Haldane Pl DD3 6 B4
Haldane St DD3 6 B4
Haldane Ter DD3 6 B4
Halford Ct KY15 25 C1
Halley Pl DD3 6 B3
Halley Ter DD3 6 B3
Hallowhill KY16 28 C5
Halyburton Pl KY15 25 B3
Hamilton Av, Dundee DD6 24 C1
Hamilton Av, St Andrews KY16 29 E5
Hamilton St DD5 18 B4
Hamilton Ter DD5 18 B4
Hampden Cl KY16 26 D3
Happyhillock Rd DD4 16 A2
Happyhillock Walk DD4 16 B2
Harbour Rd DD6 24 E1
Harbour Vw DD4 16 A5
Harcourt St DD3 14 D2
Harefield Av DD3 14 A1

Harefield Gro DD3 14 A1
Harefield Mews DD2 14 A1
Harefield Rd DD2,DD3 13 H1
Harestane Cres DD3 6 B2
Harestane Gro DD3 6 C3
Harestane Pl DD3 6 A2
Harestane Rd DD3 6 A2
Harestane Ter DD3 6 D3
Harley St DD5 17 H5
Harlow Pl DD3 14 B2
Harriet St DD4 15 F2
Harris Rd DD7 20 C5
Harris Ter DD4 7 G4
Harrison Av DD2 5 G5
Harrison Rd DD2 5 G5
Harrow St DD2 13 G5
Hastings Pl DD3 14 D1
Hatton Pl DD2 6 A6
Hawick Dr DD4 9 E6
Hawkhill DD1 3 A3
Hawkhill Ct DD1 14 C5
Hawkhill Pl DD1 3 A4
Hawthorn Gro DD4 9 F5
Hay Av DD5 19 F2
Hay Fleming Av KY16 28 B5
Hay St DD5 19 F2
Haymount Pk KY15 25 B2
Hayston Pk KY16 26 E1
Hayston Ter DD2 13 G3
Haywood Pl DD4 7 E6
Hazel Av DD2 13 F5
Hazel Dr DD2 13 F5
Hazel Gdns DD2 13 F3
Hazelhead Dr DD2 5 H4
Hazelhead La DD2 5 H5
Hazelhead Pl DD2 5 H5
Hazelhead Ter DD2 5 H4
Hazelton Way DD5 18 B3
Hazelwood Cl DD2 14 A1
Heal Ct DD3 14 A2
Heather Gdns DD3 6 C3
Heathfield Pl DD1 3 A3
Heathfield Wynd DD3 5 G3
Hebrides Dr DD4 7 F4
Hedge Rd DD3 3 C1
Helmsdale Av DD3 6 C3
Helmsdale Cres DD3 6 C3
Helmsdale Dr DD3 6 C3
Helmsdale Pl DD3 6 C3
Henderson St DD6 24 E2
Henderson Ter KY16 26 D3
Hepburn Gdns KY16 28 C5
Hepburn St DD3 14 C1
Heriot Gate DD5 18 A5
Hermitage Rd DD5 17 H5
Hermonhill Ter DD1 14 C5
Heron Rise DD4 7 F3
Herons La DD2 13 H2
High Mill Ct DD2 14 B6
High Rd DD6 23 F3
High St, Carnoustie DD7 21 F4
High St, Dundee DD1 3 D3
High St, Lochee DD2 13 H1
High St, Monifieth DD5 19 F2
High St, Newport-on-Tay DD6 23 F2
Highfield Av DD6 22 C5
Highfield Pl DD2 4 C3
Highgate Centre DD2 13 H2
Highland Chief Way DD4 7 F3
Hill Cres DD6 22 B6
Hill Park Ter DD6 22 B6
Hill Rd DD5 17 H5
Hill Sq DD3 14 D2
Hill St, Broughty Ferry DD5 17 H5
Hill St, Cupar KY15 25 B2
Hill St, Dundee DD3 14 C2
Hill St, Monifieth DD5 19 F3
Hill St, Newport-on-Tay DD6 23 E4
Hill Ter DD2 4 C3
Hillbank Gdns DD3 15 E2
Hillbank Pl DD3 15 E2
Hillbank Rd DD3 15 E2
Hillcrest Rd DD2 14 A4
Hillfield Rd KY16 26 E1
Hillpark Dr DD2 4 C2
Hillpark Pl DD2 4 C2
Hillpark Rd DD6 22 B6
Hillside Ct DD2 13 E3
Hillside Dr DD2 13 F4
Hillside Pl, Dundee DD2 13 F4
Hillside Pl, Newport-on-Tay DD6 23 G2
Hillside Rd DD2 13 F4
Hillside Ter DD2 13 F4
Hilltown DD3 3 D1
Hilltown Ct DD3 3 D1
Hilltown Ter DD3 3 C1
Hillview Rd KY16 26 E1
Hindmarsh Av DD3 15 E1
Hogarth Dr KY15 25 E3
Holly Blue Ct DD4 8 C6
Holly Cres DD5 18 A4
Holly Pk KY15 25 D2
Holly Rd DD5 18 A4
Holyrood St DD7 21 F3
Home St DD5 17 G5
Honeygreen Rd DD4 7 G5
Hope St KY16 29 E3
Horse Wynd DD1 3 E2
Horseleys Pk KY16 29 E5
Horsewater Wynd DD1 3 A3
Hospital St DD3 14 C1
Houston Ct KY15 25 C1
Howard Pl KY16 29 E3
Hudson Pl KY16 26 D4
Hunter Cres, Dundee DD2 12 B4
Hunter Cres, St Andrews KY16 26 E3
Hunter St DD1 3 A3
Huntly Pl, Dundee DD4 16 C3
Huntly Pl, St Andrews KY16 28 D5
Huntly Rd DD4 16 C3
Huntly Sq DD4 16 C3
Hutchison Ct KY16 29 F5
Hutton Pl DD5 18 A5
Hyndford Pl DD2 14 A5
Hyndford St DD2 14 A4
Inchcape Pl DD5 18 C2
Inchcape Rd DD5 18 C2
Inchcape Ter DD5 18 C2
Inchcolm Dr DD5 18 C3
Inchcolm Gdns DD5 18 C3
Inchcolm Ter DD5 18 D3
Inchkeith Av DD5 18 C3
Inchkeith Pl DD5 18 C3
Inchkeith Ter DD5 18 C3
Inchlaw KY16 26 E2
Inchyra Pl DD3 6 A2
Infirmary Brae DD3 3 A1
Inglefield St DD4 16 B2
Inglis St DD1 15 H3
Inn St DD6 24 D1
Innerbridge St KY16 27 C7
Innes Rd KY16 26 D4
Inver Ter DD2 4 A2
Inverarity Gdns DD5 19 E1
Inverary Ter DD3 14 B3
Invercraig Pl DD2 13 E1
Inverdovat La DD6 23 G3
Invergowrie Dr DD2 13 F4
Inverlaw Pl DD3 14 C3
Invermark Ter DD5 18 C4
Ireland St DD7 21 G4
Irvine Cres KY16 29 G5
Irvines Sq DD1 3 C1
Isla Pl*, Back Dykes DD6 24 D1
Isla St DD3 15 E2
Ivanhoe Pl DD4 15 H3
Ivory Pl DD5 17 F1
Jack Martin Way DD4 7 G3
Jacobson Gdns DD3 6 B2
Jacobson Pl DD3 6 B2
Jacobson Ter DD3 6 B3
Jamaica Sq DD3 15 E2
Jamaica St DD3 15 E2
Jamaica Twrs DD3 15 E2
James Arrott Dr DD2 13 E3
James Bell Wynd DD5 18 D1
James Black Pl DD2 13 E3
James Cowie Cl DD5 18 D1
James Foulis Ct KY16 28 D6
James Herald Ter DD5 18 D1
James Pl DD5 17 G6
James Robb Av KY16 29 E5
James St, Carnoustie DD7 20 C4
James St, Dundee DD3 14 D2
James St, Newport-on-Tay DD6 23 G1
James St, St Andrews KY16 29 E4
Jamie Anderson Pl KY16 29 E6
Janefield Pl DD4 15 F1
Jarvis Pl DD7 21 E4
Javelin Cres KY16 26 C4
Jedburgh Rd DD2 13 H4
Jetty La DD5 17 G6
Joan Bartlett Ho DD4 7 G6
John Coupar Ct KY16 29 E3
John Grahame Av DD4 7 F3
John Huband Dr DD2 4 B2
John Knox Rd KY16 28 C5
John St KY16 29 E3
Johnsons La DD1 3 B3
Johnston Av, Dundee DD3 14 B1
Johnston Av, Invergowrie DD2 12 B5
Johnston Ct KY16 29 F3
Johnston St DD1 3 B3
Katrine Av DD5 17 H3
Keats Pl DD3 14 C2
Keddie Pl KY15 25 B2
Keith Av DD7 21 F3
Keith Cres KY16 26 D4
Keith Pl DD4 16 C3
Kellas Rd DD4 9 F6
Kellyfield Ct DD4 8 B6
Kelso Pl DD2 13 H4
Kelso St DD2 13 H4
Kelvin St DD4 6 D6
Kemback St DD4 15 F2
Kemnay Gdns DD4 16 B4
Kemnay Pl DD4 16 B3
Kendal Av DD3 6 C4
Kenilworth Av DD4 15 H2
Kenmore Pl DD3 14 B2
Kenmore Ter DD3 14 B2
Kennedy Gdns KY16 28 D3
Kennet Walk DD3 14 D3
Kennoway Pl DD5 18 A3
Kenthall Gdns DD2 4 C2
Kerr St, Dundee DD2 13 H2
Kerr St, Newport-on-Tay DD6 23 G1
Kerrington Cres DD5 18 C4
Kerrs La DD2 13 H2
Kerrsview Ter DD4 7 E6
Kerrystone Ct DD4 7 H6
Keswick Ter DD3 6 C4
Kettins Ter DD3 5 H2
Kidston Ct KY16 29 F3
Kilberry Ct DD3 14 B2
Kilberry St DD3 14 A2
Kilbride Pl DD4 16 D1
Kilgask St DD6 23 G2
Killin Av DD3 14 B2
Kilmaron Cres KY15 25 B1
Kilmaron Loan DD5 18 B2
Kilmore Ter DD3 7 E3
Kilnburn DD6 23 G2
Kilravock Gdns DD4 8 A6
Kilrymont Cres KY16 29 G6
Kilrymont Pl KY16 29 G5
Kilrymont Rd KY16 29 F6
Kilspindie Pl DD2 5 H6
Kilspindie Rd DD2 5 H6
Kilspinie St DD2 5 H6
Kilwinning Pl DD4 16 D1
Kinbrae Ct DD6 23 F3
Kinbrae Park Gdns DD6 23 F3
Kinbrae Pk DD6 23 F3
Kinburn Pl KY16 29 E3
Kinburn Ter*, Double Dykes Rd KY16 29 E3
Kinclaven Dr DD3 5 H2
King St, Broughty Ferry DD5 17 G5
King St, Dundee DD1 3 E1
King St, Newport-on-Tay DD6 23 G2
King St, St Andrews KY16 29 E4
King St, Tayport DD6 24 D2
Kingennie Ct DD4 7 H6
Kingfisher Pl DD4 8 D6
Kinghorne Ct DD3 14 D2
Kinghorne Pl DD3 14 D2
Kinghorne Rd DD3 14 C3
Kinghorne Ter DD3 14 B3
Kinghorne Walk*, Kinghorne Rd DD3 14 D2
Kings Cross Rd DD2 14 A1
Kings Mason DD2 12 A6
Kingsburn Ct DD2 13 F1
Kingsburn Gdns DD2 13 F1
Kingsmuir Pk DD3 5 H2
Kingsway DD3,DD4 6 C5
Kingsway East DD4 16 A3
Kingsway Pl DD3 6 D6
Kingsway Ter DD3 6 D6
Kingsway West DD2,DD3 12 C2
Kingsway West Retail Pk DD3 6 B6
Kinkaldrum Pl DD3 15 E2
Kinkell Ter KY16 29 G5
Kinloch Pk, Carnoustie DD7 21 F4
Kinloch Pk, Dundee DD2 13 F4
Kinloch St, Carnoustie DD7 20 D5
Kinloch St, Dundee DD3 14 D2
Kinloch Ter DD3 14 C3
Kinloss Cres KY15 25 B1
Kinloss Dr KY15 25 B1
Kinloss Pk KY15 25 B1
Kinnaird St DD3 14 D2
Kinnear Ct KY16 27 C8
Kinneff Cres DD3 5 H2
Kinness Pl KY16 29 E4
Kinnessburn Gdn KY16 29 E4
Kinnessburn Rd KY16 29 E4
Kinnessburn Ter KY16 29 E4
Kinnettles Ter DD3 5 H2
Kinnordy Ter DD4 16 B5
Kinnoull Rd DD2 5 H6
Kinnoull St DD2 5 H6
Kinpurnie Pl DD3 14 B2
Kinrossie Ter DD3 6 A2
Kintail Pl DD5 17 H3
Kintore Pl DD5 16 D3
Kippford St DD5 18 D2
Kirk La DD1 3 E1
Kirk Rd DD6 23 E4
Kirk St DD2 13 H2
Kirk Walk DD7 21 G3
Kirk Wynd, Cupar KY15 25 C2
Kirk Wynd, Dundee DD6 24 E2
Kirkaldy Ct KY16 29 F5
Kirkbuddo Pl DD5 19 E1
Kirkconnel Ter DD4 16 C1
Kirkgate KY15 25 C2
Kirkhill*, Gregory Pl KY16 29 G3
Kirklands Pk KY15 25 B1
Kirkton Av DD3 6 C4
Kirkton Cres DD3 6 C4
Kirkton Mews DD3 6 B4
Kirkton Pl DD3 6 C4
Kirkton Rd DD3 6 B4
Kirkton Rd East DD3 6 C4
Kirkton Ter DD7 21 E4
Kirsty Semple Way DD2 12 D3
Knapdale Pl DD4 9 E6
Knowles Loan DD7 20 A4
Knox Gdns KY15 25 D4
Kyle Gdns KY16 28 B4
Laburn St DD1 3 B1
Lade Braes La KY16 29 F3
Lade Braes Walk KY16 29 E4
Ladybank Pl DD5 18 B3
Ladywell Av DD1 3 E1
Ladywynd KY15 25 C2
Laggan Gdns DD2 13 F1
Laidon Ter DD3 6 B5
Laing Pl DD3 15 E2
Laing St DD3 15 E2
Laird St, Dundee DD3 5 G2
Laird St, Monifieth DD5 19 G1
Lamberton Pl KY16 29 E6
Lambs La DD3 15 E3
Lammerton Ter DD4 7 F6
Lamond Dr KY16 29 E5
Landale Gdns KY15 25 E1
Langholm Gdns DD5 17 F4
Langlands Rd KY16 29 F4
Langlands St DD4 15 F2
Langlea Pl DD5 18 B2
Langshaw Rd DD2 5 G6
Lansdowne Ct DD2 5 H6
Lansdowne Gdns DD2 5 G6
Lansdowne Pl DD2 13 H1
Lansdowne Sq DD2 5 H6
Larch St DD1 14 C4
Larchfield Gdns DD3 5 G3
Largo Pl DD5 18 B3
Largo Rd KY16 28 D6
Lauderdale Av DD3 6 A4
Lauderdale Pl DD3 6 A4
Laurelbank DD3 3 C1
Lavender St DD4 16 C5
Law Cres DD3 14 B2
Law Rd DD3 14 C2
Law St DD3 14 C3
Law Steps DD3 14 B3
Lawers Dr DD5 18 B2
Lawers Rd DD5 18 D1
Lawhead Rd East KY16 28 C4
Lawhead Rd West KY16 28 B4
Lawhead School Wynd KY16 28 B4
Lawmill Gdns KY16 28 B5
Lawrence St, Broughty Ferry DD5 17 G5
Lawrence St, Dundee DD1 14 B4
Laws DD5 11 F3
Laws Cotts DD5 11 E2
Laws Hill DD5 11 F3
Laws Pl DD5 19 E1
Lawside Av DD3 14 B3
Lawside Rd DD3 14 B2
Lawside Ter DD3 14 B3
Lawson Pl DD3 14 D3
Lawton Rd DD3 14 C1
Lawton Ter DD3 14 C2
Laxford La DD5 17 H3
Learmonth Pl KY16 28 D5
Lebanon Ter KY15 25 C1
Ledmore Ter DD2 12 C3
Leemount La DD5 17 F4
Leith Gdns DD2 13 E2
Leith Walk DD2 12 D2
Leng St DD3 14 C2
Lennox Gdns DD2 13 F3
Leonard Gdns KY16 28 C6
Letham Pl KY16 28 B5
Lethnot Gdns DD5 18 B4
Lethnot St DD5 18 B4
Leven St DD5 18 A3
Lewis Ter DD4 7 F4
Leyshade Ct DD4 16 A3
Leysmill Cl DD7 21 G3
Liddel Rd DD2 13 F4
Liff Cres DD2 13 F1
Liff Dr DD2 4 B5
Liff Rd, Dundee DD2 13 F1
Liff Rd, Liff DD2 4 A5
Liff Rd, Muirhead DD2 4 A3
Liff Ter DD2 13 E1
Lilybank Rd DD4 15 F3
Lilybank Ter DD4 15 G3
Lime St DD2 14 A4
Linden Av DD6 23 G3
Lindores Pl DD5 18 B3
Lindsay Ct DD2 12 C4
Lindsay Gdns KY16 28 D5
Lindsay St DD5 17 H5
Linefield Rd DD7 21 G3
Linfield St DD4 16 B2
Lingard St DD7 20 D4
Links Av DD7 21 E4
Links Cres, Dundee DD6 24 F3
Links Cres, St Andrews KY16 29 E3
Links Ct DD6 24 F3
Links Par DD7 21 E5
Links Pl DD5 19 G1
Links Rd DD6 24 F3
Links Rd North DD6 24 F3
Linksfield DD6 24 E3
Linlithgow Pl DD2 12 A6
Linton Rd DD2 5 F6
Lintrathen Cl DD3 6 C6
Lintrathen Ct DD3 6 C6
Lintrathen Gdns DD3 6 B6
Lintrathen St DD3 6 C6
Lismore Ter DD4 7 G4
Lister Pl DD2 13 F4
Little Carron Gdns KY16 28 B5
Littleton Gdns DD2 4 C2
Livingstone Cres KY16 29 E4
Livingstone Pl, Dundee DD3 6 A4
Livingstone Pl, St Andrews KY16 29 E4
Livingstone Ter DD3 6 A4
Lochalsh St DD5 18 A4
Lochay Pl DD2 12 D3
Lochee Rd DD1 3 A1
Lochend Rd DD7 20 D4
Lochinver Cres DD2 12 C3
Lochlair Ct KY15 25 E3
Lochlee Ter DD4 16 A4
Lochside Cotts DD6 24 E2
Lochside Gdns DD6 24 E2
Lochty St DD7 21 F4
Lockhart Pl KY16 29 E3
Loftus Pl DD3 6 B3
Loftus Rd DD3 6 B3
Loftus St DD3 6 B3
Loganlee Ter DD2 14 A3
Logie Av DD2 14 A4
Logie Gdns DD2 14 B4
Logie St DD2 14 A2
Logies La KY16 29 F3
Lomond Dr DD7 21 G3
Lomond Pl, Dundee DD4 7 H5
Lomond Pl, St Andrews KY16 26 F1
Long La DD5 17 G5
Long Row DD7 21 H4
Long Wynd DD1 3 C4
Longcroft Rd DD4 16 B2
Longhaugh Rd DD4 8 A5
Longhaugh Ter DD4 16 A1
Longtown Ind Est DD4 16 B2
Longtown Pl DD4 16 A3
Longtown Rd DD4 16 A3
Longtown St DD4 16 B3
Longtown Ter DD4 16 A3

Loons Rd DD3 14 A2
Loraine Rd DD4 15 G1
Lorimer St DD3 14 C1
Lorne Av DD5 19 G1
Lorne Cres DD5 19 G1
Lorne St, Dundee DD2 13 G1
Lorne St, Monifieth DD5 19 G1
Lorraine Dr KY15 25 B3
Lossie Pl DD2 12 D3
Lothian Cres DD4 8 B6
Loudens Cl KY16 29 F3
Lousen Pk DD7 21 F4
Lovers La KY15 25 C2
Lower Pleasance DD1 14 C4
Lower Princes St DD1 15 F4
Lownie Rd DD7 21 G3
Lowson Av DD7 21 G4
Lucklaw Rd KY16 26 E2
Luffness Walk DD4 8 B6
Luke Pl DD5 17 G3
Lulworth Ct DD4 8 C6
Lumsden Cres KY16 28 B4
Lumsden Pk KY15 25 D3
Luna Pl DD2 12 C4
Lunan Ter DD4 16 B5
Lunardi Pl KY15 25 E3
Lundie Av DD2 14 A1
Lundie Pl DD2 6 A6
Lundin Cres DD6 24 F3
Luther Pl DD2 12 D2
Lynch Walk DD2 12 D2
Lyndhurst Av DD2 13 H1
Lyndhurst Pl DD2 5 H6
Lyndhurst Ter DD2 13 H1
Lynnewood Pl DD4 15 G1
Lyon St DD4 15 F3
Lytton St DD2 14 B5

Macadam Pl DD2 6 A5
Macalpine Rd DD3 6 A3
Macalpine Sq DD3 6 A4
Macaulay St DD3 14 D3
Macdonald Smith Dr DD7 20 B4
Machrie Pl DD4 9 E6
Mackenzie St DD7 21 F3
Maclagan Rd DD7 20 D4
Maclaren Gdns DD2 13 H2
Maclaren Walk DD2 14 A2
Macnabb Pl DD4 7 H6
Macnabb St DD4 7 G6
Madeira St DD4 15 G1
Magdalen Pl DD1 14 C6
Magdalen Yard Rd DD2 14 B6
Magdalen Yd*, Patons La DD2 14 B6
Magnum Ho*, Seagate DD1 15 E4
Main St, Balmullo KY16 26 F2
Main St, Dundee DD3 14 D2
Main St, Invergowrie DD2 12 B4
Main St, Leuchars KY16 26 C3
Main St, St Andrews KY16 27 C7
Mains Dr DD4 7 F6
Mains Loan DD4 7 F4
Mains Rd DD3 14 D2
Mains Ter DD4 7 F6
Maitland Dr KY15 25 C2
Maitland St, Dundee DD4 15 F2
Maitland St, Tayport DD6 24 E2
Malcolm Cres DD5 19 E2
Malcolm St DD4 15 F2
Malcoms Pend DD1 3 A2
Mallaig Av DD2 12 C2
Malthouse Cl DD1 3 D3
Manhattan Ct DD4 15 F2
Manor Gdns DD7 21 G2
Manor Pl DD5 17 H6
Manse Pl DD5 19 F2
Mansfield Rd KY16 26 F1
Mansion Dr DD4 7 E3
Maplewood Dr DD2 14 A1
Marchfield Cres DD2 14 A5
Marchfield Rd DD2 14 A5
Marchfield Ter DD2 13 H5
Margaret Cres DD5 16 D5
Marine Dr DD5 19 G2
Marine Par, Dundee DD1 3 F3
Marine Par, Tayport DD6 24 D1
Marine Pl KY16 29 G3
Mariner Dr DD2 12 C4
Mariner St DD7 21 H4
Marionfield Pl KY15 25 D3
Market Pl DD6 24 D1
Market St, Dundee DD1 15 G3
Market St, St Andrews KY16 29 E3
Marlee Ct DD5 17 H3
Marlee Pl DD5 18 A3
Marlee Rd DD5 17 H3
Marryat St DD3 14 D1
Marryat Ter DD3 14 D1
Mars Gdns DD6 22 D4
Marshall St DD2 13 H2
Martin St DD4 7 G6
Martingale Gdns DD4 15 F3
Mary Ann La DD1 3 E2
Mary Slessor Sq DD4 15 F3
Marybank La DD2 13 G1
Maryfield La DD5 17 H5
Maryfield Rd DD5 17 H5
Maryfield Ter DD4 15 F1
Masons La DD6 24 D1
Matthew Ct DD1 14 C4
Mauchline Av DD4 16 A3
Mauchline Pl East DD4 16 A2
Mauchline Pl West DD4 16 A2
Maule St, Broughty Ferry DD5 18 C3
Maule St, Carnoustie DD7 21 E4
Maule St, Monifieth DD5 19 F3
Mavis Haugh KY16 28 C5
Maxwell Town Twrs DD3 15 E3
Maybole Pl DD4 16 D1
Mayfield Gro DD4 15 H2
Mayfield La DD7 21 E4
Maynard Rd KY16 28 D5
Mayo Av DD2 13 G6
McDonald St DD3 14 D3
Mcduff Dr DD6 24 E1
McGill Rd DD7 21 H3
McGill St DD4 15 F2
McGonagall Sq DD2 14 B6
McGregors Bldgs KY16 27 C8
McInnes Gdns KY15 25 D1
Mcintosh Hall*, Abbotsford Cres KY16 29 E3
Mcintosh Patrick Pl DD5 18 D2
Mckenzie Sq KY16 28 B5
McKinnon St DD3 14 D3
McLean Pl DD3 6 A2
McLean St DD3 6 A2
McManus Ct DD4 7 H6
McVicars La DD1 14 C5
McWalters Flds KY16 26 F1
Meadow Entry DD1 3 D2
Meadow La DD1 3 D2
Meadow Rd KY16 26 C3
Meadowside DD1 3 D1
Meadowside Rd KY15 25 D3
Mears Ct KY16 26 D4
Megginch Gdns DD4 8 B6
Melbourne Pl KY16 29 E3
Melfort Pl DD3 7 E3
Melrose Ter DD3 15 F1
Melville Ct DD6 24 D2
Melville La DD1 15 G3
Melville Ter DD2 13 H5
Menteith St DD5 17 H3
Menzieshill Rd DD2 13 E5
Mercat Wynd KY16 29 F3
Mercury Way DD2 13 H6
Mericmuir Gdns DD3 6 A4
Mericmuir Pl DD3 6 A4
Merton Av DD2 13 H1
Meteor Row KY16 27 C5
Methven Av DD2 14 A2
Methven St DD2 13 H2
Methven Walk DD2 14 A2
Mid Bonvil KY15 25 B2
Mid Craigie Ind Est DD4 16 A3
Mid Craigie Rd DD4 16 A3
Mid Rd DD3 14 D2
Mid Wynd DD1 14 C5
Middle Rd DD2 4 B5
Middlebank Cres DD2 14 A5
Middlefield Brae KY15 25 D1
Middleshade Rd KY16 28 C4
Middleton Cres DD4 7 F3
Midmill Rd DD4 16 A2
Mill Brae DD5 19 F3
Mill Ct DD6 24 E2
Mill La DD6 24 E2
Mill Rd, Barry DD7 20 A4
Mill Rd, Invergowrie DD2 12 B4
Mill St DD5 18 A6
Millar St DD7 21 E4
Millbank KY15 25 B3
Millbank Pk KY15 25 C3
Millbay Gdns DD2 12 D5
Millbay Ter DD2 12 D4
Millers Wynd DD1 14 C5
Millfield KY15 25 B3
Millgate KY15 25 C3
Millhall Cres DD2 13 F5
Millhill DD5 19 E3
Miln St DD1 3 A2
Milnbank Gdns DD1 14 B4
Milnbank Rd DD1 14 B4
Milner St DD4 7 G6
Milnes East Wynd DD1 14 C4
Milton of Craig Rd North DD4 16 B3
Milton of Craig Rd South DD4 16 B3
Milton Pk DD5 19 E3
Milton Pl DD5 19 E3
Milton St, Dundee DD3 14 C1
Milton St, Monifieth DD5 18 D4
Miltonbank Cres KY16 27 C6
Minard Cres DD3 14 C3
Mintlaw Pk DD5 16 D3
Minto Pl DD2 14 A5
Mitchell St DD2 14 B4
Moathill East KY15 25 C2
Moathill Rd KY15 25 B2
Moffat Rd DD4 16 B3
Moir Cres KY16 28 C6
Molison St DD4 15 F2
Moncur Cres DD3 14 D1
Monifieth Rd DD5 18 A5
Monkton Loan DD4 16 C1
Montague St DD5 18 C3
Montgomerie Av DD4 16 B4
Montgomerie Cres DD4 16 B4
Montgomery Ct KY16 28 C5
Montpellier Gdns DD4 9 E6
Montrave Av KY15 25 B2
Montrave Pl DD5 18 A3
Monymusk Rd DD4 16 C3
Moonzie Bank KY15 25 B3
Morar Pl DD5 18 A3
Morgan Pl DD4 15 G2
Morgan St DD4 15 F2
Morlich Gdns DD5 18 A4
Morris Pl DD2 12 B5
Mortimer St DD3 14 C2
Morton Cres KY16 28 B5
Morven Ter DD2 14 A3
Mosquito Dr KY16 26 C4
Mossgiel Cres DD4 7 H6
Mossgiel Pl DD4 7 H6
Motray Cres KY16 27 C6
Motray Pk KY16 27 C6
Mount Pleasant DD1 14 C5
Mount Stewart Rd DD6 22 B6
Muir Gdns KY16 28 B4
Muirfield Cres DD3 6 B5
Muirfield Pl DD3 6 C6
Muirfield Rd DD3 6 C6
Muirfield St DD3 6 C6
Muirfield Ter DD3 6 C5
Muirhead Pl DD4 17 F1
Muirnwood Pl DD5 19 F2
Muirside Ter DD5 17 G3
Muirton Rd DD2 14 A2
Mull Ter DD4 7 G4
Mulligan Ct DD2 13 H2
Munro Pl DD2 5 G6
Murray Ct KY16 26 F1
Murray Pk KY16 29 F3
Murray Pl KY16 29 F3
Murray Row KY16 26 F1
Murray St DD4 16 A5
Murrayfield Dr DD4 16 B1
Murrayfield Gdns DD4 16 B1
Murrayfield Pl DD4 16 B1
Murrayfield Rd KY16 28 C4
Murrayfield Ter DD4 16 B1
Murraygate DD1 3 E2
Murroes Pl DD5 11 F6
Muttoes Ct KY16 29 F3
Muttoes La KY16 29 F3
Mylnefield Rd DD2 12 C5
Myrekirk Rd DD2 12 D1
Myrekirk Ter DD2 12 D1
Myrtle Ter, Newport-on-Tay DD6 23 G2
Myrtle Ter, Tayport DD6 24 D1
Myrtlehall Gdns DD4 9 E6

Nairn St DD4 7 G6
Napier Dr DD2 5 F6
Napier Pl DD2 5 F6
Napier Ter DD2 5 G6
Naughton Pl DD2 13 G4
Naughton Rd DD6 22 B6
Navarre St DD5 18 C4
Neddertoun Vw DD2 4 A5
Neish St DD3 15 E2
Nelson La DD6 24 E2
Nelson St, Dundee DD1 15 E3
Nelson St, St Andrews KY16 29 E4
Nelson St, Tayport DD6 24 E2
Nelson Ter DD1 15 E3
Nesbitt St DD4 15 G2
Nethergate DD1 3 B4
Nethergate Bsns Centre DD1 3 D4
Netherlea Pl DD6 23 E4
Netherton Ter DD2 13 F2
Nevay Ter DD2 13 G3
Nevill St DD3 6 C6
Nevis Pl DD5 17 H3
New Inn Entry DD1 3 D2
New Rd DD5 18 A6
New St DD6 24 D3
Newhall Gdns DD2 13 F5
Newmill Gdns KY16 28 D5
Newport Rd DD6 24 A1
Newton Cres DD7 21 F3
Newton Rd, Carnoustie DD7 21 E3
Newton Rd, Dundee DD3 6 D3
Newtown KY15 25 C1
Newtyle Rd DD2 4 A1
Nicholl Pl DD7 21 F2
Nicholls Av KY16 26 E4
Nicholson Cotts KY15 25 B1
Nicoll St DD1 3 C2
Nicolls La DD2 13 H1
Ninewells Av DD2 13 E5
Ninewells Ct DD2 13 E3
Ninewells Dr DD2 13 E3
Nithsdale Av DD3 6 A4
Nobel Ct DD2 12 C1
Nobel Rd DD2 12 C1
Nobel Way DD2 12 C1
Noble Av DD2 12 C5
Noran Av DD4 16 A4
Norman Vw KY16 26 D4
Norrie St DD5 18 A5
Norries Rd DD7 21 H4
North Balmossie St DD5 18 C2
North Bank St DD5 19 E3
North Brown St DD7 20 D4
North Burnside St DD7 20 D4
North Castle St KY16 29 G3
North Ellen St DD3 15 E2
North Erskine St DD4 15 F2
North George St DD3 14 D2
North Isla St DD3 15 E2
North Lindsay St DD1 3 C3
North Marketgait DD1 3 B1
North Ramsay St DD5 19 G1
North Somerville Pl DD3 14 D3
North St, Dundee DD3 14 D2
North St, St Andrews KY16 29 E3
North Ter DD6 22 C5
North Union St, Cupar KY15 25 C2
North Union St, Dundee DD5 19 F2
North Wellington St DD3 15 E2
North William St DD3 15 E2
Northfield Rd DD6 23 G1
Northview Ter DD6 22 B6
Northwood Ct DD5 17 F4
Norwood DD6 23 G2
Norwood Cres DD2 13 G5
Norwood La DD6 23 G2
Norwood Ter DD2 13 H5
Nursery Rd DD5 17 H4

O'Neill Ter DD4 16 A2
Oak Vale KY15 25 E2
Oakley Pl DD5 17 H5
Ogilvie Ct DD5 17 F5
Ogilvie Rd DD5 17 E5
Ogilvie St DD4 15 F2
Ogilvy Pl DD6 24 E3
Ogilvy St DD6 24 D2
Old Craigie Rd DD4 15 H1
Old Glamis Rd DD3 6 D6
Old Hawkhill DD1 3 A4
Old Kings Cross Rd DD3 14 A2
Old Mill Est DD1 3 B2
Old Muirton Rd DD2 13 H2
Old St Andrews Rd KY16 27 D8
Old Station Rd KY16 28 D2
Old Toll Loan DD4 9 F6
Orchard Ct DD4 7 F3
Orchardgate KY15 25 C2
Orleans Pl DD2 13 E3
Ormiston Cres DD4 8 B6
Orrin Pl DD2 13 E3
Osborne Pl DD2 14 B6
Overgate Shopping Centre DD1 3 D3
Overton Gdns DD2 13 F2
Oxford St DD2 13 G4

Palais Ct DD1 3 C3
Palmer Pl DD2 4 C2
Palnackie Rd DD5 18 D2
Panbride Pl DD7 21 G3
Panbride Rd DD7 21 F2
Panbride St DD7 21 G3
Panbride Vw DD7 21 G2
Panmure Ind Est DD7 20 D5
Panmure St, Broughty Ferry DD5 18 A5
Panmure St, Carnoustie DD7 20 D4
Panmure St, Dundee DD1 3 D2
Panmure St, Monifieth DD5 19 G2
Panmure Ter, Broughty Ferry DD5 18 B4
Panmure Ter, Dundee DD3 14 C3
Panmurefield Rd DD5 18 D3
Panmurefield Ter DD5 18 D3
Paradise Rd, Dundee DD1 3 C1
Paradise Rd, Monifieth DD5 19 E2
Park Av, Carnoustie DD7 21 F4
Park Av, Dundee DD4 15 F2
Park Homes DD7 21 E5
Park Pl, Dundee DD1 3 B3
Park Pl, Lochee DD2 13 H2
Park Rd, Dundee DD3 6 C6
Park Rd, Invergowrie DD2 12 B5
Park St, Dundee DD1 14 C4
Park St, St Andrews KY16 29 F4
Park Vw, Dundee DD5 19 F1
Park Vw, St Andrews KY16 26 E1
Park Wynd DD1 3 A3
Parker St DD1 3 B1
Parkhead Pl DD4 16 A2
Parkhill Bsns Centre*, Park St DD1 14 C4
Parkhill Pl DD5 17 H3
Parliament Sq KY15 25 C2
Pasteur La DD2 13 F4
Paterson St DD3 14 C1
Patons La DD2 14 B6
Patrick Blair Pl DD2 13 E4
Patrick Pl DD2 14 B6
Pearce Av DD5 17 F2
Peddie St DD1 14 B4
Peebles Dr DD4 9 E6
Peel St DD2 13 H2
Peep O Day La DD1 15 F3
Pennan Gro DD5 16 D3
Pennycook La DD1 14 B5
Pentland Av DD2 14 A4
Pentland Cres DD2 14 A4
Perrie St DD2 13 G2
Perth Rd, Dundee DD2 12 C4
Perth Rd, Invergowrie DD2 12 A4
Peter Arbuckle Pl DD2 12 B5
Peter St DD1 3 E2
Peterburn Ter DD2 12 C2
Philip St DD7 21 F4
Pilmour Links KY16 29 E2
Pilmour Pl KY16 29 E2
Pinewood Gdns DD2 14 A1
Pipeland Rd KY16 29 E5
Pipeland Walk KY16 29 E5
Piper St DD4 16 D1
Pitairlie Rd, Dundee DD4 16 A2
Pitairlie Rd, New Bigging DD5 11 F1
Pitalpin Ct DD2 5 G6
Pitalpin St DD2 13 G1
Pitcairn Dr KY16 26 E2
Pitcairn Pk KY16 26 D4
Pitcairn Rd DD3 6 A2
Pitcaple Walk DD4 8 B5
Pitcur St DD3 6 A2
Pitempton Rd DD3 6 A1
Pitfour St DD2 14 B4
Pitkerro Ct DD4 7 H6
Pitkerro Dr DD4 7 H5
Pitkerro Rd DD4 15 G2
Pitlessie Gdns DD3 6 B2
Pitlethie Rd KY16 26 D3
Pitreavie Pl DD3 6 B2

Pitroddie Gdns DD3 6 A2
Pitscottie Rd KY15 25 D2
Pitskelly Ind Site DD7 20 C4
Pitskelly Rd DD7 20 C3
Playfair Dr, Dundee DD3 6 B5
Playfair Dr, St Andrews KY16 26 E4
Playfair Ter, Dundee DD3 6 B5
Playfair Ter, St Andrews KY16 29 E3
Pleasance Ct DD1 14 C4
Plockton Ter DD2 12 D2
Polepark Rd DD1 14 B4
Pond La DD6 24 E2
Poplar Dr DD4 9 F5
Poplar Grey Ct DD4 8 C6
Portmore Pl DD2 13 F1
Portpatrick Ter DD5 18 D2
Portree Av DD5 18 A4
Post Box Rd DD2 4 C2
Powrie Pl DD1 15 E3
President Grant Pl DD6 24 D1
Priestden Pk KY16 29 G5
Priestden Pl KY16 29 G5
Priestden Rd KY16 29 G5
Prieston Rd DD3 6 D3
Primrose Bank DD4 16 C5
Primrose St DD7 20 D4
Princes St, Dundee DD4 3 F1
Princes St, Monifieth DD5 19 G2
Priory Ct DD4 7 H6
Priory Gdns KY16 28 D5
Promenade DD6 24 E2
Prospect Pl DD3 3 B1
Prospect Ter DD6 23 G1
Provost Black Dr DD6 24 C1
Provost McGowan Pl DD2 14 B6
Provost Niven Cl KY16 29 E4
Provost Rd, Dundee DD3 14 D1
Provost Rd, Tayport DD6 24 D2
Provost Scott Ct KY16 25 C2
Provost Wynd KY15 25 C2
Provosts Walk DD5 19 E1
Pullars Cl DD1 3 D2

Quarry Gdns DD2 13 G1
Quarry Knowe DD2 13 G1
Quarry Rd, Dundee DD2 4 B2
Quarry Rd, St Andrews KY16 26 E1
Quarryfield Ct DD4 8 B6
Quarryside DD2 13 G1
Queen St, Broughty Ferry DD5 17 G5
Queen St, Carnoustie DD7 21 F3
Queen St, Dundee DD1 3 E1
Queen St, Monifieth DD5 19 F2
Queen St, Newport-on-Tay DD6 23 G2
Queen St, Tayport DD6 24 D3
Queens Bldgs DD6 24 D1
Queens Ct DD5 17 H5
Queens Gdns KY16 29 F3
Queens Ter KY16 29 F4

Radernie Pl KY16 28 B5
Raglan St DD4 15 F3
Railway Pl KY15 25 D2
Ralston Mt DD5 16 D5
Ralston Pl DD5 16 D5
Ralston Rd DD5 16 D4
Ramsay St, Broughty Ferry DD5 18 A5
Ramsay St, Monifieth DD5 19 G1
Rankine Ct DD6 22 D4
Rankine St DD3 14 B3
Rankines Ct DD1 3 D2
Rannoch Ct DD3 6 A4
Rannoch Pl DD3 6 A4
Rannoch Rd DD3 6 A5
Rannochmoor Gdns DD3 6 A2
Rattray Pl DD5 19 E2
Rattray St, Dundee DD1 3 C2
Rattray St, Monifieth DD5 19 E3
Ravensby Park Gdns DD7 20 B4
Ravensby Rd DD7 20 B5
Ravenscraig Gdns DD5 17 E5
Ravenscraig Pl DD2 13 E2
Ravenscraig Rd DD2 13 E2
Red Admiral Ct DD4 8 C6
Redcastle Cres DD5 17 G3
Redcroft Pl KY16 26 D4
Redford Pl DD5 19 F1
Redmyre Gdns DD4 16 B5
Redwood Av DD2 14 A1
Reform St, Dundee DD1 3 D2
Reform St, Monifieth DD5 19 G2
Reform St, Tayport DD6 24 D2
Regent Pl DD5 17 F5
Reid Gdns KY16 28 C6
Reid Sq DD3 14 D2
Reid St DD3 14 D2
Reids La DD2 13 G1
Rennell Rd DD4 15 H1
Reres Gdns DD5 18 B4
Reres Rd DD5 18 A5
Reresmount Pl DD5 18 B5
Rescobie Av DD4 16 B4
Reservoir Rd DD6 22 B6
Rhynie Rd DD5 17 E3
Richmond Ct DD2 14 A5
Richmond Ter DD2 14 A6
Riddell Ter DD4 7 H5
Riggs Pl KY15 25 D2
Ritchie Av DD5 19 F1
Ritchies La DD2 14 B5
River Cres DD2 13 E5
River Ter KY16 27 C6
Riverside App DD2 14 B6
Riverside Av DD2 12 B3
Riverside Bsns Pk DD2 13 E6
Riverside Ct DD2 13 G6
Riverside Ct Ind Est KY15 25 D2
Riverside Dr DD2 13 F6
Riverside Gdns DD6 22 C4
Riverside La DD6 23 E4
Riverside Pl DD2 13 E5
Riverside Rd DD6 22 B5
Riverview Dr DD5 19 G3
Robert St DD6 23 G2
Robertson Rd KY15 25 D3
Robertson St DD4 15 F3
Robson St DD4 15 H2
Rockfield Cres DD2 14 A5
Rockfield St DD2 14 A5
Rockwell Pl DD3 14 C1
Rodd Rd DD4 15 H1
Rolands Wynd DD6 24 E2
Roodyards Rd DD1 15 H3
Rose La, Dundee DD3 14 D3
Rose La, St Andrews KY16 29 F3
Rose St, Carnoustie DD7 21 E4
Rose St, Tayport DD6 24 E2
Roseangle DD1 14 C6
Rosebank Pl DD3 14 D3
Rosebank Rd DD3 14 D3
Rosebank St DD3 14 D2
Rosebank Ter DD3 14 D3
Roseberry St DD2 14 B3
Roseburn Gdns DD4 8 B6
Rosedale Cres DD5 18 C3
Rosefield Pl DD1 14 B4
Rosefield St DD1 14 B4
Rosehall Gdns DD2 12 C3
Rosemarkie Cres DD5 18 C3
Rosemarkie Pl DD5 18 C3
Rosemount Cres DD2 4 C2
Rosemount Rd, Birkhill DD2 4 C2
Rosemount Rd, Dundee DD2 5 G4
Rosewood Ter DD2 13 H5
Roslin Gdns DD4 15 H1
Ross Gdns DD2 13 G2
Ross Rd KY16 26 D4
Ross Ter DD5 19 F1
Rossie Av DD5 17 F3
Rothes Pk DD5 16 D3
Roundhill Rd KY16 29 F6
Roundyhill DD5 19 E2
Rowanbank Gdns DD5 18 A5
Rowantree Cres DD4 7 H5
Roxburgh Ter DD2 13 H5
Royal Exchange La DD1 3 D2
Rugby Ter DD5 18 A5
Russell Cres DD4 16 A2
Russell Pl DD3 14 D2
Rustic Pl DD1 3 C1
Rutherford Rd DD2 5 H5
Ruthven Pl KY16 28 D5
Ruthven Rd DD4 16 C3
Ruxton Pl DD7 21 E4
Ryehill La DD1 14 B5

Saggar St DD2 14 A3
St Albans Ter DD3 5 H3
St Andrews La DD1 3 E2
St Andrews Pl DD1 3 E1
St Andrews St DD1 3 E1
St Ann St DD2 13 H2
St Boswells Ter DD3 5 H3
St Bunyans Pl KY16 26 C3
St Catherine St KY15 25 D2
St Clement Pl DD3 5 G2
St Clement Ter DD3 5 G2
St Columba Gdns DD3 5 H3
St Davids La DD1 3 B3
St Dennis Pl DD3 5 G2
St Dennis Ter DD3 5 G2
St Edmund Pl DD3 5 G3
St Edmund Ter DD3 5 G3
St Fillans Rd DD3 5 G3
St Fillans Ter DD3 5 H3
St Fort Pl DD6 22 D4
St Fort Rd DD6 22 D4
St Giles Pl DD3 5 H3
St Giles Ter DD3 5 H3
St Gregorys*, Gregory La KY16 29 G3
St Johnswood Ter DD2 13 H5
St Kilda Pl DD3 5 H3
St Kilda Rd DD3 5 G3
St Kilda Ter DD3 5 H3
St Leonard Pl DD3 6 A3
St Leonard Rd DD3 6 A3
St Leonard Ter DD3 6 A3
St Leonards Rd KY16 28 D4
St Lukes Rd DD3 6 B3
St Martin Av DD3 5 H1
St Martin Dr DD3 5 H1
St Mary Pl DD1 14 B4
St Mary St, Dundee DD1 14 C4
St Mary St, St Andrews KY16 29 G4
St Marys La, Dundee DD2 13 H2
St Marys La, Newport-on-Tay DD6 23 F2
St Marys Pl KY16 29 E3
St Marys Rd DD3 6 A3
St Mathews La DD4 15 G3
St Michaels Dr KY15 25 D3
St Monance Pl DD3 5 G3
St Mungo Ter DD3 5 H3
St Nicholas Pl DD3 5 G3
St Nicholas St KY16 29 G4
St Ninian Pl DD3 5 G3
St Ninian Ter DD3 5 G3
St Peter St DD1 14 B5
St Phillans Pl DD6 23 G2
St Regulus Hall*, Queens Gdns KY16 29 F4
St Regulus Rd DD5 19 E1
St Ronans Av DD4 15 H3
St Roques La DD1 3 F1
St Salvador St DD3 15 E2
St Vincent Ct DD5 17 H6
St Vincent St DD5 17 H6
Salem St DD1 3 C1
Salton Cres DD4 8 B6
Samson Pl DD7 20 D4
Sandeman Pl DD3 15 E1
Sandeman St DD3 14 D1
Sandhaven Gdns DD5 16 D3
Sandy Herd Ct KY16 29 F5
Sandyhill Cres KY16 29 F4
Sandyhill Rd, Dundee DD6 24 D3
Sandyhill Rd, St Andrews KY16 29 F5
Sandylands Rd KY15 25 C4
School Brae KY16 26 D3
School Dr DD3 6 B5
School Hill KY16 26 D3
School Rd, Dundee DD5 11 F1
School Rd, St Andrews KY16 26 E1
School Wynd, Muirhead DD2 4 A2
School Wynd, Tayport DD6 24 E2
Scooniehill Rd KY16 29 E6
Scotscraig DD6 23 F3
Scotscraig Cres DD2 5 G4
Scotscraig Ct DD2 5 H4
Scotscraig Dr DD6 24 B1
Scotscraig Gro DD2 5 H4
Scotscraig La DD2 5 G4
Scotscraig Pl DD5 18 A3
Scotscraig Rd DD2 5 G4
Scotscraig St DD2 5 H4
Scotstarvit Vw KY15 25 B3
Scotston Gdns DD4 16 C4
Scotswood Cres DD6 22 C5
Scotswood Ter DD2 13 H5
Scott Cres DD6 24 B1
Scott St, Dundee DD2 14 A4
Scott St, Newport-on-Tay DD6 23 G2
Scott Way DD5 17 F2
Scrimgeour Pl DD3 3 A1
Seabourne Gdns DD5 18 B5
Seabrae DD7 21 G4
Seabraes Ct DD1 14 C6
Seabraes La DD1 3 B4
Seacraig Ct DD6 23 G2
Seafield Cl DD1 14 C6
Seafield La DD1 14 C6
Seafield Rd, Broughty Ferry DD5 17 G5
Seafield Rd, Dundee DD1 14 C5
Seafield Ter DD5 17 G4
Seaforth Cres DD5 16 D4
Seaforth Rd DD5 16 D4
Seagate DD1 3 E2
Selkirk Gdns DD4 9 E6
Servite Ct, Dundee DD5 19 F2
Servite Ct, St Andrews KY16 26 D4
Servite Ct*, Patons La DD2 14 B6
Session St DD1 3 B3
Seymour Av DD2 14 B5
Seymour St DD2 14 A4
Shaftesbury Ct DD2 14 A5
Shaftesbury Pk DD2 14 A5
Shaftesbury Pl DD2 14 A5
Shaftesbury Rd DD2 14 A5
Shaftesbury Ter DD2 14 B5
Shamrock St, Carnoustie DD7 21 E4
Shamrock St, Dundee DD4 15 F1
Shanwell Ct DD6 24 E3
Shanwell Ct Ind Est DD6 24 F3
Shanwell Rd, Carnoustie DD7 21 E3
Shanwell Rd, Tayport DD6 24 E3
Shanwell Rd South DD6 24 F3
Sharps Ct DD2 13 H2
Sharps La DD2 13 G2
Shelley Gdns DD3 14 C2
Shepherds Brae DD6 23 F3
Shepherds Loan DD2 14 B5
Shepherds Rd DD6 23 F3
Sherbrook Cres DD3 6 C5
Sherbrook Gdns DD3 6 C5
Sherbrook Pl DD3 6 C5
Sherbrook St DD3 6 B5
Shields Av KY16 29 G4
Shiell Ct DD5 18 B5
Shiell St DD5 18 B5
Shoolbraids KY16 29 F6
Shore Ter DD1 3 E3
Shorehead KY16 29 G3
Short La KY15 25 C2
Sibbald St DD3 15 E2
Sidlaw Av, Dundee DD3 5 H2
Sidlaw Av, Dundee DD3 5 G2
Sidlaw Ct DD3 6 A2
Sidlaw Gdns DD2 4 B2
Sidlaw Ter DD2 4 C2
Silport Pl DD7 20 C5
Silver Button Yd DD4 7 F3
Silver Link Av DD4 8 D6
Simpson Av DD2 13 F4
Simpson Ct DD2 13 E4
Simpson Pl DD7 21 E4
Sinclair St DD2 13 H1
Skene St DD5 17 H3
Skinners Steps KY15 25 C1
Sloan St KY16 29 E4
Small Copper Ct DD4 8 C6
Small Meadow Ct DD4 8 C6
Smalls La DD1 3 B4
Smalls Wynd DD1 3 A3
Smeaton Rd DD2 12 D1
Smellies La DD1 3 A1
Smieton Ct DD7 20 D4
Smieton St DD7 20 D4
Smillie Ct DD3 3 B1
Smith St DD3 6 C6
Smithy La KY16 26 F1
Smithy Rd KY16 26 E1
Soapworks La DD1 3 C1
Solway Gdns DD5 18 D2
Somerville Pl DD3 14 D3
Somerville Pl East DD3 14 D3
Soutar St DD3 6 C6
Souterrain DD5 11 G4
South Baffin St DD4 15 G3
South Balmossie St DD5 18 D4
South Bri KY15 25 D2
South Castle St KY16 29 F3
South Ct KY16 29 F3
South Dr DD2 4 B6
South George St DD1 15 E3
South Kingennie Steadings DD5 10 B3
South Kinloch St DD7 21 E5
South Marketgait DD1 3 E4
South Ramsay St DD5 19 G2
South Rd, Cupar KY15 25 C4
South Rd, Dundee DD2 12 C2
South Rd, Liff DD2 4 A6
South St, Dundee DD5 19 G2
South St, St Andrews KY16 29 F3
South Tay St DD1 3 B3
South Taymouth St DD7 21 E5
South Union St KY15 25 C2
South Victoria Dock Rd DD1 3 F3
South Ward Rd DD1 3 B3
Southampton Pl DD4 16 C5
Southampton Rd DD4 16 C5
Southfield KY16 29 E4
Southgait Cl KY16 29 F3
Sowerby Pl DD3 6 B4
Soyaux Av DD5 19 F1
Spartleton Pl DD4 9 E6
Spearshill Rd DD6 24 D1
Speckled Wood Ct DD4 8 C6
Speed St DD2 14 A5
Spence Gdns DD5 17 G6
Spence Pl DD5 17 G6
Spencer Cres DD7 21 G3
Spey Dr DD2 12 D3
Spinkie Cres KY16 28 D6
Spinners Wynd DD2 14 B6
Spitfire Pl KY16 26 C4
Spottiswoode Gdns KY16 28 D5
Springfield DD1 14 C5
Springhill DD4 15 G3
Springhill Gdns DD4 15 G3
Staffa Pl DD2 6 A5
Stanley Rd DD5 17 G4
Stannergate Rd DD1 15 H3
Station Brae DD6 23 G2
Station Cres DD2 12 B5
Station Path DD6 23 E4
Station Rd, Barry DD7 20 A4
Station Rd, Carnoustie DD7 21 G4
Station Rd, Cupar KY15 25 D2
Station Rd, Invergowrie DD2 12 B5
Station Rd, St Andrews KY16 27 C5
Station Ter DD2 12 C5
Step Row DD2 14 B5
Stevens Yd DD2 14 B6
Stevenson St DD2 13 H1
Stewart St, Broughty Ferry DD5 17 H4
Stewart St, Dundee DD2 13 H1
Stewart Ter DD5 19 G1
Stewarts La DD2 13 G1
Stirling Ct DD3 14 D2
Stirling St DD3 14 D2
Stirling Ter DD3 14 D3
Stobsmuir Rd DD4 15 G1
Stobswell Rd DD4 15 F2
Stonehouse Bsns Centre KY16 29 E5
Stracathro Ter DD5 18 B4
Strachan Av DD5 16 D3
Straiton Ter KY16 26 E2
Straiton Wynd KY16 29 E5
Strathaird Pl DD2 12 C3
Strathaven Ter DD4 16 C1
Strathbeg Pl DD5 18 A3
Strathblair Av DD6 22 A6
Strathcarron Pl DD2 12 D3
Strathdee Ter DD5 16 D4
Strathdon Pl DD5 16 D4
Stratheden Rd DD5 16 D4
Strathern Rd DD5 16 D4
Strathisla Rd DD5 16 D4
Strathkinness High Rd KY16 28 A3
Strathkinness Low Rd KY16 28 A4
Strathmartine Rd DD3 6 A2
Strathmore Av DD3 14 B1
Strathmore Pl DD5 18 C3
Strathmore St, Broughty Ferry DD5 18 B4
Strathmore St, Dundee DD3 15 E1
Strathspey Pl DD5 16 D4

Strathtay Rd DD5 16 D4
Strawberry Bank DD2 14 B5
Strips of Craigie Pl DD4 16 B4
Strips of Craigie Rd DD4 16 B4
Striven Pl DD5 18 A3
Strome Ter DD5 18 B4
Struan Pl DD6 23 G2
Struan St DD6 23 G2
Sugarhouse Wynd DD1 3 E1
Summerfield Av DD4 8 C6
Summerfield Gdns DD4 16 C1
Summerfield Ter DD4 16 C1
Summerhill KY16 26 E1
Sunadale Ct DD4 9 F6
Sunart Pl DD5 18 A3
Sunart St DD5 18 A3
Sunnybrae Ter DD3 6 B4
Sutherland Cres DD2 13 G2
Sutherland Pl DD2 13 G2
Sutherland St DD2 13 H2
Swallow Apts DD5 19 F3
Swallowtail Ct DD4 8 C6
Sycamore Pl DD2 14 A4
Sylvan La DD6 23 G2
Symers St DD3 6 A3

Taits La DD2 14 B5
Tannadice Ct DD3 15 E1
Tannadice St DD3 15 E1
Tannery Ct KY15 25 C1
Tarbert Pl DD2 13 F3
Tarves Pk DD5 16 D3
Tarvit Av KY15 25 D3
Tarvit Ct KY15 25 E2
Tarvit Dr KY15 25 E2
Tarvit Gdns KY15 25 E2
Tay Ct DD5 19 G2
Tay Road Bri DD1 3 F3
Tay Sq DD1 3 C4
Tay St, Monifieth DD5 19 G2
Tay St, Newport-on-Tay DD6 23 F2
Tay St, Tayport DD6 24 D1
Tay Street La DD1 3 C4
Tay Ter DD6 23 G1
Tayfield Pl DD2 14 B6
Taylor St DD2 13 H1
Taylors La DD2 14 B5
Taymouth Pl DD5 18 A5
Taymouth St DD7 21 E5
Taymouth Ter DD7 20 C5
Taypark DD5 17 F5
Taypark Ter DD6 24 D2
Tayport Rd DD6 23 G1
Tayside St DD7 21 G4
Tayview Dr DD2 4 B5
Tayview Rd DD2 4 B5
Tayview Ter DD6 23 G1
Telford Rd DD2 5 H5
Temple La DD1 3 B3
Templeton Rd DD3 4 D1
Tennis Rd DD7 21 F3
Tentsmuir Pl DD5 18 A3
Terrace La DD7 21 F4
Terrace Rd DD7 21 E4
Teviotdale Av DD3 6 A3
The Aspens DD4 8 B5
The Barony KY15 25 C2
The Beeches DD4 8 B5
The Canongate KY16 29 E4
The Cedars DD4 8 B5
The Croft KY16 26 D4
The Elms DD4 8 B5
The Esplanade DD5 18 A6
The Fairway DD5 19 G1
The Forum DD1 15 E4
The Hawthorns DD4 8 B5
The Hazels DD4 8 B5
The Lane DD2 4 C2
The Larches DD4 8 B5
The Links KY16 29 E2
The Maples DD4 8 B5
The Mount KY16 26 E1
The Neuk DD2 12 A6
The Old Dairy DD5 17 H4
The Pends KY16 29 G3
The Pines DD4 8 B5
The Poplars DD4 8 B5
The Rowans DD4 8 B6
The Scores KY16 29 E2
The Shore DD2 12 A6
The Spruces DD4 8 B5
The Stables DD5 19 F1
The Stack Leisure Pk DD2 13 H1
The Steading KY16 29 H4
The Wellgate Shopping Centre DD1 3 D1
The Willows DD4 8 B5
Thirlestane Pl DD4 9 E6
Thistle La KY16 29 E3
Thistle St, Carnoustie DD7 21 E4
Thistle St, Dundee DD3 14 D2
Thomas Cl DD3 5 H1
Thomas Ct DD7 20 C5
Thomas Maclagan Way DD2 13 E3
Thomas St DD7 20 C5
Thomas Wise Pl DD2 13 F4
Thomastoun Dr KY15 25 E1
Thompson Av DD7 20 C4
Thomson St DD1 14 B6
Thornbank Ct DD4 15 G2
Thornbank Pk DD4 15 G3
Thornbank St DD4 15 G3
Thornbank Ter DD4 15 G3
Thornton Rd DD3 6 D3
Thorter Neuk DD1 15 G4
Thorter Row DD1 15 F4
Thurso Cres DD2 12 D3
Thurso Gdns DD2 12 D3
Tiger Beach Dr DD7 20 C5
Tighnduin Gdns DD5 19 F2
Tillycairn Pl DD4 8 B6
Tircarra Bank DD5 18 B5
Tircarra Gdns DD5 18 B5
Tircarra Pl DD5 18 B4
Tofthill DD2 13 H1
Tofthill Pl DD2 13 H1
Toll Rd KY16 27 C5
Tom Johnstone Rd DD5 17 F3
Tom Mcdonald Av DD2 12 D4
Tom Morris Dr KY16 29 E5
Tom Stewart La KY16 29 E5
Tommy Armour Pl DD7 20 C5
Torridon Rd DD5 18 A4
Torwood Pl DD4 8 A5
Tower Ct DD5 16 D5
Trades La DD1 3 E2
Traill St DD5 17 G4
Tranent Gdns DD4 8 B6
Tranent Gro DD4 8 B6
Tranent Walk DD4 8 B6
Traquair Gdns DD4 9 E6
Travebank Gdns DD5 19 F2
Trinity Pl KY16 28 C5
Troon Av DD2 5 3
Troon Cres DD2 5 3
Troon Gdns DD2 5 4
Troon Pl DD2 5 H3
Troon Rd DD2 5 G3
Troon Ter DD2 5 4
Trottick Mains DD4 7 E3
Tullideph Pl DD2 14 A3
Tullideph Rd DD2 14 A3
Tullideph St DD2 14 A3
Tulloch Ct DD3 3 C1
Tulloch Pl KY16 28 C6
Tummel Pl DD2 13 F3
Turnberry Av DD2 5 G4
Turniehill Gdns DD2 4 C2
Turriff Pl DD3 6 A4
Turriff St DD3 6 A4
Tutor Cl KY16 26 D4
Tutor Rd KY16 26 D4
Tuttle Cl KY16 26 E4
Tweed Cres DD2 13 E2
Twynholm Gdns DD5 18 D2
Tyndall Cres DD5 18 D4
Tyndall Pl DD5 18 D3

Uist Ter DD4 7 G4
Ullapool Cres DD2 12 C2
Ulverston Ter DD3 6 C4
Union Bank DD2 13 H1
Union Pl, Dundee DD2 14 B5
Union Pl, Newport-on-Tay DD6 23 G2
Union St, Broughty Ferry DD5 17 H6
Union St, Dundee DD1 3 D3
Union St, Monifieth DD5 19 F2
Union St, Newport-on-Tay DD6 23 G2
Union St, St Andrews KY16 29 F3
Union Ter DD3 14 D3
University of Dundee DD1 3 A4
Upper Constitution St DD3 14 C2
Upper Dalgairn KY15 25 C1
Upper Victoria Link DD7 20 A1
Ure St DD1 14 C5
Urquhart St DD1 14 C4

Valgreen Ct DD4 16 A2
Vernonholme Est DD2 13 F6
Viaduct Walk KY16 29 E4
Victoria Gdns DD5 17 F4
Victoria Rd, Broughty Ferry DD5 17 F5
Victoria Rd, Dundee DD1 3 D1
Victoria Rd, Tayport DD6 24 D1
Victoria St, Carnoustie DD7 20 D4
Victoria St, Dundee DD4 15 F3
Victoria St, Monifieth DD5 19 F1
Victoria St, Newport-on-Tay DD6 23 G3
Viewmount Rd DD6 22 B6
Viscounts Pend DD4 7 F4
Vorlich Av DD5 18 C2
Vorlich Dr DD5 18 C1

Wade St DD2 4 C6
Walker Pl KY16 28 B4
Walker St DD5 18 A6
Walkers Mill DD3 15 E2
Wallace Av KY16 29 E4
Wallace St, Carnoustie DD7 20 D4
Wallace St, Dundee DD4 15 F3
Wallace St, St Andrews KY16 29 E4
Walrond St DD4 15 G1
Walton Pk*, Blackness Rd DD1 14 C4
Walton St DD1 14 C4
Ward Rd DD1 3 B2
Wardlaw Gdns KY16 29 E3
Wards Av DD7 20 D4
Warrack St KY16 29 G5
Warren Pl DD2 4 C2
Warwick Cl KY16 26 D3
Waterend Rd KY15 25 D2
Waterside DD5 19 E3
Waterside Vw DD7 21 H3
Waterson Crook DD6 23 E4
Watson Av KY16 29 F4
Watson St DD4 15 G3
Watts Gdns KY15 25 E1
Waverley Ter DD4 15 H3
Weavers Loan DD3 14 D3
Weavers Yd DD4 15 F3
Wedderburn Pl DD3 14 D1
Wedderburn St DD3 14 D1
Well Park Ter East DD6 23 E4
Well Park Ter West DD6 23 E4
Well Pl KY15 25 D1
Well Rd DD1 14 C5
Well St, Cupar KY15 25 D1
Well St, Dundee DD5 19 G2
Wellbank La DD2 14 A2
Wellbank Pl DD5 19 G2
Wellburn St DD2 13 G1
Wellgate Shopping Centre DD1 15 E4
Wellgate St DD6 23 E4
Wellgrove St DD2 13 G1
Wellington Sq DD3 15 E2
Wellington St DD1 15 E3
Wellington Twrs DD3 15 E2
Wemyss Cres DD5 18 D3
Wemyss Gdns DD5 18 A2
Wessex Av KY16 26 D4
West Acres KY16 28 B4
West Acres Dr DD6 22 D4
West Bell St DD1 3 B2
West Burn La KY16 29 F3
West Dennison Rd DD4 15 G1
West Grange Rd DD5 18 D1
West Grange St DD5 19 E2
West Green Park Sales Centre DD2 4 B5
West Grove Av DD2 13 G5
West Hendersons Wynd DD1 3 A2
West Lyon St DD4 15 F3
West Marketgait DD1 3 B2
West Park Rd DD2 13 H4
West Park Villas DD2 13 H5
West Path DD7 21 E4
West Pitkerro Ind Est DD5 17 F1
West Port, Cupar KY15 25 B2
West Port, Dundee DD1 3 B3
West Port Pl KY15 25 B2
West Queen St DD5 17 G5
West Rd DD6 23 E3
West Sands Rd KY16 29 E1
West School Rd DD3 6 A5
West Smieton St DD7 20 D4
West Somerville Pl DD3 14 D3
West St DD3 14 C1
West Victoria Dock Rd DD1 3 F3
West Wynd DD1 14 B5
Westbarn Rd DD5 18 C4
Westcroft Pl DD4 16 A2
Westcroft Rd DD4 16 A2
Wester Gourdie Ind Est DD2 4 C6
Wester Gourdie Walk DD2 5 E6
Westerton Av DD5 17 H3
Westfield Av, Cupar KY15 25 B2
Westfield Av, Dundee DD1 14 C5
Westfield La DD1 14 C5
Westfield Pl, Carnoustie DD7 20 C5
Westfield Pl, Dundee DD1 14 C5
Westfield Rd, Cupar KY15 25 A3
Westfield Rd, Dundee DD5 17 G5
Westfield St DD7 20 C4
Westfield Ter DD6 23 E4
Westhall Ct DD4 7 H6
Westhaven Pk DD7 21 H3
Westhaven Rd DD7 21 G2
Westpark Gdns DD2 13 H5
Westpark Rd, Cupar KY15 25 B2
Westpark Rd, Dundee DD6 23 E4
Westview KY16 29 F3
Westwater Pl DD6 22 C5
Westwood Ter DD6 23 F4
Wetherby Pl DD3 14 B1
Whalers Cl DD4 15 F2
Whinfield Pl DD6 23 G2
Whinny Brae DD5 17 H5
Whirlwind Pl KY16 26 C4
Whistlers Way DD3 15 E3
Whitburn Pl DD3 6 B2
Whitefauld Rd DD2 13 E5
Whitehall Cres DD1 3 D4
Whitehall St DD1 3 D3
Whitehill Ter KY16 29 E4
Whitenhill DD6 24 E2
Whitfield Av DD4 16 B1
Whitfield Ct DD4 8 B6
Whitfield Dr DD4 8 B6
Whitfield Gdns DD4 16 B1
Whitfield Loan DD4 16 C1
Whitfield Rise DD4 16 B1
Whitfield Shopping Centre DD4 8 B6
Whitfield Sq DD4 16 B1
Whitfield Ter DD4 16 C1
Whithorn Pl DD5 18 D2
Whittet Ct DD2 14 B5
Whittle Pl DD2 5 E6
Whortbank DD2 14 A2
Whorterbank DD2 14 A2
Wilkies La DD1 14 C5
William Barclay Sq DD3 3 D1
William Fitzgerald Way DD4 7 F3
William Lammond Cres DD5 18 D1
William Payne Ct DD6 24 E3
William Pl DD7 21 G4
William St, Carnoustie DD7 21 G4
William St, Dundee DD1 15 E3
William St, Newport-on-Tay DD6 23 G2
William St, Tayport DD6 24 D1
Willison St DD1 3 C3
Wimberley Ct DD5 17 F4
Wimberley Hos DD2 13 F4
Windmill Rd KY16 29 E3
Windsor Ct, Broughty Ferry DD5 17 G5
Windsor Ct, Dundee DD2 14 A5
Windsor Gdns KY16 28 C6
Windsor Pl DD2 14 B6
Windsor St DD2 14 B5
Windsor Ter DD2 14 A5
Winram Pl KY16 28 D6
Winter Pl DD7 21 G4
Winthank Ct*, Kirk Wynd KY15 25 C2
Wishart Archway DD1 3 F1
Wishart Gdns KY16 29 F6
Wishart Pl DD1 3 E1
Wishart St DD3 14 C2
Wiston Pl DD2 13 H1
Wolseley St DD3 15 F2
Wood La DD5 19 E1
Wood Rd DD2 4 C3
Woodbine Ter DD6 23 G2
Woodburn Pl KY16 29 G4
Woodburn Ter KY16 29 G4
Woodburne St DD4 16 A4
Woodhaven Av DD6 22 D4
Woodhaven Pl DD5 18 B3
Woodhaven Ter DD6 22 D4
Woodlands Ter DD4 7 E6
Woodlands Way DD2 12 A6
Woodlea Gdns DD7 21 E3
Woodmuir Cres DD6 23 E4
Woodmuir Ter DD6 23 E4
Woodside Av DD4 7 F6
Woodside Ter, Carnoustie DD7 20 D4
Woodside Ter, Dundee DD4 7 E6
Woodville DD5 17 E4
Woodville Pl*, Forfar Rd DD4 15 F2
Wortley Pl DD4 15 G1
Wright Av DD2 13 E6
Wurzburg Ct DD2 12 D3
Wyvis Av DD5 18 B2
Wyvis Pl DD5 18 B2
Wyvis Rd DD5 18 B2

Yarrow Ter DD2 13 F3
Yeaman St DD7 21 E4
Yeamans Alley DD2 13 H1
Yeamans Ct DD2 13 G2
Yeamans La DD2 13 G2
Yeamans Shore DD1 3 D4
Yewbank Av DD5 18 B5
Young Av DD2 4 B2
Young Ct DD6 24 C1
Younger Gdns KY16 28 A5
Youngsdale Pl DD6 23 G2